THIS IS WYOMING LISTEN...

Edited By:
Roberta C. Cheney
and
Emmie D. Mygatt

Written By:
Wyoming Writers

Published By:
BIG HORN BOOKS
Basin, Wyoming 82410

THIS IS WYOMING
LISTEN...

International Standard Book Number: 0-89100-002-X
Library of Congress Catalog Card Number: 77-2624
Big Horn Book Publishing Company
211 South 4th Street, Basin, WY 82410
©1977 By Roberta C. Cheney and Emmie D. Mygatt
First Edition Published 1977
Printed in the United States

Published By:
Big Horn Books
Basin, Wyoming 82410

PREFACE

A good story should have colorful characters, an interesting background and an intriguing situation. Wyoming has the colorful characters, an interesting and varied background, and is in the midst of an intriguing situation that will shortly affect its own future and have an impact on the nation.

It was to portray and preserve the unique facets of Wyoming today that this book was undertaken by Wyoming Writers and is therefore a picture of our state as seen by Wyomingites. The intent of the book is to make a reader feel Wyoming, see how it looks, how it smells, and above all—how its people think and live.

We can find out about Yesterday in an armchair or in the library, but writers have to run to catch Today. They know that what is happening now will be an exciting chapter in tomorrow's history. Too much of what the nation needs lies under our soil to have it otherwise. Twenty-five percent of the nation's known coal deposits lie beneath this surface. Water is too scarce to meet the needs of large scale mining and industry and maintain ranching as well. What will happen, only the future can tell. In this book we have barely touched on the subject of coal, including only enough material to give a feeling of what it is like to live and work on land you have owned for years, only to realize that now its use could be taken from you because you do not own the mineral rights on the fields where your cattle graze.

We have tried to record the transient NOW in poetry, fiction, pictures, and factual articles. Our Wyoming scenery ranges from bleak to incredibly beautiful; our population averages out to 3.6 persons per square mile. This amount of space breeds character and independence and most of us, with all our hearts, would like to keep it that way. We know we cannot, so we have chosen to record what goes on in our mountains, plains, and meadow-land.

We felt the best balanced book would be a collection of stories, poems, and articles that begin in history but place chief emphasis on warm and human portrayal of modern Wyoming. The book will be regional in scope, but we hope that the feeling it arouses will have a universal appeal.

The Editors

THIS IS WYOMING — LISTEN

TABLE OF CONTENTS

I Am the West, Discover my Dreams

Pete Fetsco
Sheridan

Photo Courtesty of Archie Nash

I am the West . . .
Maker of men; breaker of hearts and
possessor of that dream which has always
challenged all mankind—
that there is something important to see
on the other side of a hill;
something worthwhile to be seen
from the other side of the mountain.

I am what
the man who first wrote the word "freedom"
was thinking about, and I stand here
dedicated to the proposition
that all which was good in man did not die
in some past generation
but grows daily
in each succeeding people who stop here.

The Bridgers, Bakers, Carsons—
all of them were here and before them,
a proud people who walked tall on the land
and developed a lineage which boasted
such names as Red Cloud, Crazy Horse, Washakie.

These are gone;
so are the times of quiet fury and
sudden bloodshed
as men fought desperately to possess
what little of me they could in a lifetime.

And still I stand here.
My mysteries have not been blunted
for those of you who care to look for them;
my challenge still holds for those
who care to do more than
blink by in a steel-wrapped cocoon.

I shun
the claustrophobes who need concrete towers
and acrid air to prove their existence.
I welcome
those who just naturally have a "why?"
tucked into their disposition somewhere that
they just always have to ask.

I was born fiercely,
amid upheaval,
fire, flood and drought,
and yet today I pose challenges
to those who pass this way.

But if you would find splendor
of any sort—awesome moutains; quiet
valleys; rushing rivers and quiet stream;
burning desert and lush grass,
then you have arrived, and
have only to sample what you see around you.

If you still have
the ability to dream
of what can be while cherishing that which
has been; walk the mountainside;
stand where heroes stood before you
and listen to their dreams.

If you seek
to find yourself,
find me first.
I will show you the way.
Sit a spell, partner.
You haven't seen anything yet.

Reprinted from
Sheridan Press

When I took notions to ride the grub-line for a spell, I usually tried to pick ranches that bachelors owned. Women, lots of times seemed too fussy. I felt more at home where there was just bachelors.

That's why I happened to be stayin' at Link Morrison's place, helpin' with the chores and odd jobs, to sort of pay for my board.

Link was an old timer. He'd been around here and there since God made little kittens, so he knew lots of stories to tell, and he liked a new face around now and then to tell them to.

So one day when a couple of riders from the H-Bar and one from the Lazy-B stopped by, Link began tellin' about his days up in the gold camps.

"When Gold City was boomin'," he said, "there was more strange characters around that you could round up in all the rest of the Territory if you took a month. Characters, you know, is just individuals that don't fit in anywhere, so they congregate in places where they don't feel hemmed in.

"Now a funny thing about guys like that is that often as not, they can't git along with other people, and lots of times not even with theirselves.

"But Loco Sam and Hardrock Pete was different. They got along real good. They was pardners and had a minin' claim a ways up the gulch from where their cabins was. It wasn't much of a claim as minin' claims go, but they had high hopes for it. Every now and then a speck of color would show, and they knowed they was on the verge of hittin' Old Lady Luck herself.

"Their cabins was close together. Loco's was a little uphill from Hardrock's, and there was a woodshed between them that both of them used. It had two doors. The uphill door was Loco's and the downhill door was Hardrock's. With that kind of arrangement they figgered there'd be no cause for misunderstandin'.

"They was a curious pair, all right. Loco was tall and skinny and had a sparse growth of scraggly salt-and-peper whiskers that growed like half-dead quakers* on a southside slope. But Hardrock was short an' stocky with a long body an' short legs. And his whiskers was as black as the inside of their minin' tunnel. He always kept them trimmed like a circuit judge's.

"Now the reason they lived apart like they did was because Hardrock didn't like the way Loco kept house. Loco was a mite untidy. Besides he had a predeliction of every now and then goin' into town and havin' a few too many rounds at the local Saloon. Hardrock didn't approve of that.

A Game of Chess

Thomas Connell
Lander

Illustration Courtesy of Joan Malone

*Quaking Aspens

"But like it or not, Hardrock usually got involved. For sure as a snail will crawl, everytime Loco went on a bender, someone would come a runnin' for Hardrock to go git that crazy Loco before he tore the saloon up, and coax him back to his rat's nest.

"But misunderstandin' finally come between 'um. Why is real hard to say. Maybe it was too much winter. And maybe it was the last game of chess.

"You see, Loco loved to play chess. He was the undisputed champeen of Gold City, and in a way that went to his head. He thought he couldn't be whipped. Anyway he taught Hardrock to play and every now and then when the day's work was over he would go down to Hardrock's cabin, or sometimes Hardrock would climb up to his, and they would have a game. Loco always won, and he liked to rib Hardrock about it. He got pretty rough at times, too."

At that point, Link goes over to the stove and lifts the lid to stuff some more wood in and poke at the flame. Then he comes back wipin' his droopy moustache, and grins.

"You see," he says, "Loco likes the winnin' more than the game. Maybe it was because that was the only thing he could beat Hardrock at. Anyway he liked to watch Hardrock flounder along and make mistakes that he could remind Hardrock of, and point them out.

"But there was one way he always catered to Hardrock. When he was down to Hardrock's, he didn't spit his tobacco juice at the stove, or on the floor, like he did in his own place. No sir! He took a can along for his spittin' because old Hardrock was mighty fussy about his cabin.

"Maybe the reason they stayed pardners so long was because Hardrock was really a generous cuss and if'n you didn't mess up his cabin he could tolerate a lot of monkeyshines.

"Well anyway Hardrock begins to git onto the game after a while and little-by-little begins to make it harder for Loco to win. Before the winter was over it was nip and tuck lots of times. Loco quits laughin' so much and his remarks git meaner and meaner.

"Now you can't keep sayin' mean things to a feller without it finally rubbin' his hide. Even if old Hardrock did seem serene he's really all set to blow up at the right moment.

"Finally one day Loco goes into town and gits a snoot full, and feelin' mighty high as he heads back to his cabin, he decides to git the chessboard and whip the pants off'n old Hardrock.

"Well, the game gits goin' and instead of Loco winnin' like he usually did, he finds Hardrock checkin' every move he makes. The fun has gone out of the game and Loco begins to git mad. Then he gits so upset he makes a real bad move and he's lost the game.

"So Loco sort of rares up and says, 'Well, chess-head, we'll play one more game an' we'll see who wins that!' Then he reaches for the spittin' can that's on the table besides him and accidently knocks one of Hardrock's fancy keep-sake dishes off'n the table.

"That's the fuse that sets old Hardrock off. He was real proud of them dishes and set a heap of store by them. He kinda raises up, and the whiskers on his face stand out like quills on a porkypine. 'Now you done it! Now you done it!' he says. 'You old whiskey soak! Yore as clumsy as a bull moose in a willer patch!'

"Loco wipes the tobacco juice off'n his chin and says 'Dammit, ya old fool, it's only a cup!

" 'Only a cup, ya say!' Hardrock has stood up so fast that he's knocked chessmen and chess board all over the floor. 'Only a cup! My Grand Mammy's china cup! and you say it's only a cup! Why you blatherin' idjet! You ain't got no more sense than a yappin' coyote!'

"Loco says then 'Maybe I'm a yappin' coyote, but I don't have a lot of fancy dishes around like some old maid. Besides, I think yore slick fingered!'

"Now Loco knows that Hardrock won't cheat, but he's so mad, he don't care. He just wants to discredit Hardrock any way he can.

"Hardrock gits really mad then. He shakes a fist under Loco's nose. 'You stand in my cabin an' call me a cheat? Why you stringy misbegotten bag of buzzard bait! I always knowed yore mammy belonged on the street. An your Pappy just happened by! I've seed more refinement in my Gran' Daddy's old gray sow!''

"Loco's face turns as red as dogwood in September. He turns and stomps from the room and he don't need no lantern to light the way.

"They go to work the next morning, though, but they don't talk to each other. Loco says first thing, 'Hardrock, don't you say nothin' to me cause I ain't talkin' to you.' And Hardrock says, 'I won't, you ornery old jackass!'' It goes like that for a couple weeks, without either of um sayin' boo to the other, except to grunt as signals when they was needed.

"Now something like that is bound to break sooner or later, and the break comes when Loco decides to fill up on Kentucky Rye, so he heads into town.

4

"But the drinks don't do much good. He's still boilin' inside when he totters back to his cabin. Thinkin' about it he decides he will really git even with that Hardrock in a way he won't fergit.

"He's brought a bottle back with him to sort of tide him over so he takes a big swig and weaves down to the woodshed.

"There he takes a piece of wood that looks about right and carries it back to his cabin. Then he gits a augur and bores a hole right down the middle of it. He has a little trouble doin' this 'cause he's a trifle unsteady, but he gits it done. Then he fills the hole with black blastin' powder, makes a stopper for it and carries it down to the woodshed. He figgers to leave his surprise where Hardrock will pick up.

"In the meantime he finds his reinforcements gone, and he's taken by a chill. Well the only thing to do then is go git his bottle. But when he gits to his cabin, he finds the bottle empty. That means another trip to town.

"He gits to town and he's just got to tell somebody about the trick he's played on old Hardrock. While he's recuperteratin' from his chill, he tells Mac Highboard, his drinkin' chum about it.

"What he don't know though, is that while he's in town, Hardrock has gone up for some wood and sees the stick Loco has put in there for him. It ain't layin' straight like his own wood. It's layin crossways. He figgers it's one of Loco's that has got there by mistake. So he takes it back to Loco's side of the shed and leaves it there.

"Well, after a bit Loco figgers he's well enough to git back to his cabin. But on the way the chill hits him again. It seems the only thing for him to do is git back there as quick as he can, build a good warm fire and crawl into his soogans.

"When he gits there the fire's plumb out and all his firewood is gone, so he has to go down to the shed to git some. He grabs the first sticks he comes to and heads back to his quilts. He gits a good fire goin' and flops into bed. But he aint no more than got covered up when there's the loudest explosion you ever heard. The stove is blowed apart, the windows is knocked out, and the cabin is so full of smoke you couldn't push your way through it.

"Well, I'm headin' that way when I hear the explosion. Old Mac has told me about Loco's trick, and I figgered maybe I could git there before Hardrock gits ahold of them sticks. But I'm a little late. It's Loco's bailiwick that explodes, not Hardrock's.

"Hearin' the noise, Hardrock comes poundin' up the trail. He's a-hollerin' 'Loco! Loco! My God, Loco!'

"A couple of other characters from down the gulch a ways come a-runnin' too. When they git there they see Hardrock standin' open-jawed in the doorway, with pieces of stove and pans and dishes scattered all around him. And inside on the bed they can hear old Loco thrashin' around and blubbering' like a two-year-old with colic.

"Hardrock says, then 'My God! Old Loco's gone plumb looney! If'n I knowed losin' that game was goin' to make him do this I'd of let him win!' "

Illustration Courtesy of Joan Malone

"I'd gone down to the river to fish. There was a good pool I knew. I'd caught a three-pound brook trout in it some days before, and now in the yellow afternoon, with a brooding lightning storm building over the mountains, I sniffed fish rising. Usually I float the river, but this time I walked, out across the sagebrush to a loop of willows. There's a steep bank here, and with careful casting, you can get a fly to the riffles and the reverse current beyond. The water just below me was black-deep and cold.

In addition to my rod, I'd taken a 20-gauge shotgun. I'd noticed a badger up in this area and hoped to kill him. The reason simply, is that the badger digs large holes that you can't see when you are galloping after calves in the sagebrush. If a horse steps into one, he can break a leg or hurt his rider. Badgers, ground squirrels and skunks are pretty much the extent of my big-game hunting. Often, though, after seeing a dog come in with a mouth full of quills, I debate adding porcupine to the list.

But this afternoon I didn't find a badger or anything else. I set my shotgun down in the willows and moved slowly along the steep bank, casting out into the river. Engrossed as I was, in the whip of the fly and the constantly changing unkown of the water, I never thought to look around at the bank, the heavy jungles of willows. I imagined once or twice that I'd heard branches rubbing in the wind.

I Met a Moose

Otis Carney
Cora

Reprinted by permission by the author and Random House publisher

Photo Courtesy of Vacationland Studio

Photo Courtesy of Vacationland Studio

Then I knew I'd heard something. I whirled. A face was behind me, about fifteen feet back in the willows. It was moving toward me, silently, a few inches at a time. I sucked a sharp breath. The face was a moose we call Gladys. Her big yellow teeth were bared, lips drooping down, and her hair raised like knives on her shoulder hump.

I did a quick measurement. A couple of steps backward and I'd be in the river. I couldn't run past her. About thirty feet to my right, along the bank, I'd propped my empty shotgun in a willow.

I started toward it, a slow step first, then walking quicker. The willows began to crash. Gladys came after me, flinging out her big sharp hooves, her whole body sagging and grunting at every angry step. I ran then, snatched up the gun, my fingers fumbling into my pocket, dropping one shell into the river, getting the other into the chamber snapping it shut. Then I stopped and looked back. She was still a dozen feet away, beginning to paw, her head low, ready to charge.

"Gladys!" I hollered. "Goddamn you!"

I didn't want to shoot her, and I wasn't too sure that one 20-gauge shell would do much good. Because this was a tough moose. The winter before, she'd attacked a cowoy at the neighboring ranch. She'd waited for him at night, when he walked out of the cookhouse to go to his trailer. After she'd charged him twice in a row, he hauled out a 12-gauge shotgun and shot her in the face. He blinded her in one eye, and that was how I recognized her. But the next morning she was still around. She attacked the cowboy when he was out feeding his cattle. He threw hay hooks into her side, and that drove her down to Dave Shannon, who was on the sleigh, feeding our cattle. At times Dave carries a rifle on the sleigh, but didn't have it then. Gladys charged him, knocked the team off the hard-packed snow trail and they floundered in five-foot drifts, tangling in their harness. She took on Dave's cattle dogs, and finally drifted away. But right after we'd come to the ranch, she appeared outside our window one morning. She trotted around the house, stomped, peered in until we thought she was going to smash the widows. Maybe it's the reflection or just sheer cussedness, but moose have been known to charge houses too.

As this flashed through my mind, Gladys and I were locked in a stare-down on the bank of the river. I couldn't decide what to do. Then, behind her in the willows, I caught a glimpse of reddish brown...two ears. Four ears. They came wobbling out, her twin calves, big as Shetland ponies but not very old. I was aware that she'd seen them, exposing themselves, and now I knew that the moment had come. This was when she'd put me in the river. As she started toward me, grunting, I reached down, picked up a stick and flung it at her, then a rock, another stick. I kept hollering at her, backing away so I wouldn't have to shoot her. But I was running out of ground now. There was a steep bank I had to go up. When I got close enough to it, I turned tail and scampered up that bank. Gladys followed to the bottom and glowered at me. I threw some more stones at her, and finally she nudged her calves back into the willows. Then she stood defiantly in the center of my fishing hole, and I didn't go back down. I left that piece of country to her, from then on.

7

We moved to Jackson Hole, Wyoming, in 1948—a decade before it was introduced nationally on a First-Name-Only basis.

It was late May, and like everyone who approaches the valley from the south, we dropped down from what seemed like endless sagebrush desert, with mountains so distant one felt they were only imaginary to an expansive green hole in the earth's crust velveted with thousands of acres of thick conifers, steep craggy cliffs cut by winding whitewater and smooth fragrant pine grass right out of *Bambi*. Elk, deer, and moose crossed the narrow winding road at will, and mountain sheep could be observed on the high rocky bluffs.

Some fifty miles later, coming into town, there were no billboards, no used-car lots, no service station, and no rhyming Burma Shave signs. There were only meadows overcome with Springtime, Hereford cattle that hardly had to lower their heads to eat, Meadowlarks in chorus, and those awesome mountains that seemed to jut straight up from the valley floor.

There were just the three of us—Mother,

Save a Green One for Me

Marcia W. Hoffman
Jackson

Photo Courtesy of A.K. Wogensen

Daddy, and me, and Jackson Hole was to be our new home. Daddy had found us an apartment and our furniture was arranged there, but we would be spending the summer at a Ranger Station called Goosewing which, he told us, was 40 miles north and east of the town of Jackson and on the Gros Ventre (pronounced Grow Vaunt) Ranger District of the Teton National Forest.

Forty miles was one thing; forty miles "up the Gros Ventre" was quite another. Twenty miles of that road was a car-and-three-fifths wide, which was ok if your three-fifths happened to be on the mountain side. But if you had the bad luck to be going the other way, it was straight down 200 feet to the river below and, all in all, a pretty humbling

experience. People who knew the country drove with one eye on the road and the other on the sky, for if one drop of rain got on that clay soil, a chemical impossibility occurred, and the road became so well lubricated that as you slid uncontrollably around those hairpin turns, you prayed to God to get stuck.

The Gros Ventre Ranger Station was almost at the end of the line—in fact it *was* the end of the telephone line. Two longs and a short would get the ranger and anyone else who wanted to hear the news first-hand. There were a few ranches on further up the river, but it was about 10 miles downstream to the nearest neighbor, and 30 miles to the closest electric power line.

9

The house sat on a hill with a timbered backdrop and looked out over the Gros Ventre River and a lot of the 502,000 acres that made up Daddy's district. The barn and corral were right behind, and immediately became a favorite hangout. The government, I learned, had 12 horses, some saddle horses, some pack horses, and two roan work horses. We had a horse of our own too, a white freckled gelding named Dusty with just enough Arabian blood to make him a snob. Right off the bat, Daddy hired me on (gratis) as the Morning Wrangler, a title that made me feel positively indispensable to the entire United States Department of Agriculture.

Morning was always my preferred time of day anyway, and morning "up the Gros Ventre" was the best it could ever be. The air was spicy with pine and sage and the hardy little phlox that grew somehow right out of the dry white soil; the colors where sharp and alive, and the wild Geranium still held a sip of sparkling dew in its throat. The Lower Pasture, as we called it, was a hodgepodge of terrain. It had hills with patches of Quaking Aspen, some flat stretches of sagebrush; it had a deep, narrow gulley that channeled a step-across creek, and a mountainside or two of lodgepole pine. The Upper Pasture was steeper and mostly timbered and it was from here one could look way up the river as it wound through the budding green willows and glistened in the sun. Here also, one could find wild strawberries and Columbine to take home to one's Mother.

So off I would go, certain that I had the best job in the world, bridle in one hand, a bag of oats in the other, listening for the faint sound of the horsebell. Chances are I would pick a different horse each morning to ride back so they could all get their turn at scaring me half to death. As soon as I would bridle and jump on, all hell would seem to break loose with the horses vying for the first place on the trail, a good share of kicking, biting and professional jealousy, and finally—the mad-dash race for the corral. There was no holding the wrangle horse in, either, as he was upset enough at the thought of necessarily coming in last. It was a wild and woolly event, and the kind of thing one didn't tell one's Mother if one wanted to keep one's job!

The four saddle horses were all nice animals to ride, and I decided that it would be a good plan to take one for a brisk little run every day. We would walk slow and easy about two miles up or down the road, with me talking and the horse listening (twitching his ears forward and back), and then at about the same spot, I'd lean forward on his

neck and away we'd go, at the best speed he had, our manes flying horizontal in the wind, for the corral and that little bonus of oats I'd give him for showing me such a fine time. Daddy used to wonder what was wrong with his packstring when he'd be coming home from eight days on the trail—at a certain spot in the road, he would say, it was like "someone fired the gun and opened the gate!"

If there were mosquitos, I don't remember them, although I do remember Mother splashing 6/12 after me as I went out the door with fishing pole in hand. If there was one place I could pursue my powers of concentration it was at the old fishin' hole. And the Gros Ventre, and even the tiny tributary streams, were alive with trout. If I couldn't catch my limit of 12 in two hours—then it was a mighty poor fishing day.

The more I learned my way around that summer, the more I loved the area. I must have had some dormant hermit genes in my composition because in all my life I have never felt so content as I did roaming around those hills, admiring the rugged beauty, and visiting with God. Mother had a ruling that I had to report home every two hours which put a distinct fence in my exploring territory, but I was, after all, her only one and just 11, so every two hours it was. Mother was a master on her wood stove, turning out daily wonders like homemade cottage cheese and crusty golden loaves of bread, but she baked chocolate cakes and oatmeal cookies regularly too—to help ease the pain of my two-hour return.

Each day of the summer was much like every other—except Saturday. Mother had another ruling that everyone, including wranglers, fishermen, and mountain explorers, must clean his room come Saturday morning. My bedroom was really 1/4 room, being approximately 4' x 10', just large enough for a cot, a drawer for underwear, and a closet big enough to accommodate a change of levis and a shirt. It was precisely that time in my life I decided that women's work was not for me. But regardless of my "druthers," I cleaned the room. On the other hand, Daddy gave me 10 cents a time for cleaning the barn which meant shoveling out four stalls of you-know-what, sweeping the grain room and the ramps—and I thought this was a privilege afforded only to competent Head Wranglers. I also enjoyed carrying in the wood because there was a family of chipmunks living in the woodpile who would come out and tell me what they would like from the cookie jar.

In those days, a ranger's work involved getting

right out on the district, and there were few roads, so Daddy and I began packtripping together. Besides the two horses we rode, we would take two or three pack horses, depending on how long we planned to be gone. We would ford the river and follow a tributary stream to the place where it would trickle, cold and tasty, out of the ground. Then possibly we would follow another drainage to its head before we camped the night. We'd unload the pack, hobble the horses, pitch the tent, fetch the water, and start our little campfire blazing. Then, without fail, Daddy would dutifully attempt to teach me how to construct supper. Somehow he felt I could not survive in the wilderness if I did not learn to cook. I simply did not have time for that—not when there was cutthroat in the creek and the sun was low in the sky.

"If you would just learn one thing," he would persist, "and that is how to make a cream gravy. A cream gravy is so versatile. You can put canned meat into it and pour it over mashed potatoes. You see, it takes three ingredients to make gravy—just three: grease, flour, and liquid. Now you see how easy that is?"

"Yes, but Daddy," I would squirm impatiently, "if we're going to have fish for supper, I've *got* to get *out* there—"

You know, I never did learn how to make gravy until I was married. But I was one whale of a fisherman!

Those were beautiful times—all of them. I have pictures in my mind and memories so special, they will last me all my life. If all children everywhere could have at least one summer like that, I can't help but feel it would make such a good difference in the world tomorrow. There is a healing balm in the wilderness that I have found nowhere else, and when the buzz of daily living begins to wear, I have yet only to shut my eyes to flashback to some sweet moment: the sound of rushing water as I snuggle for the night in my sleeping bag, the utter, unbelievable quiet on the ridge above timberline, moonlight benevolent on the meadow, the silhouette of the horse at dusk, the smell of coffee and bacon in the morning—to regain my perspective.

I was never afraid. Sometimes I was excited when a packhorse would lose his footing on a steep shalerock grade, or a young horse would

Photo Courtesy of A.K. Wogensen

decide to lie down and roll in the river. Some of the most excitement I can recall would involve a sudden electrical storm which would drive us—pronto—into the deep timber or a gully under our horses' bellies for shelter. For moments it would seem as though the whole earth were in danger of destruction as the thunder rolled over us And lightning crackled on every side. But just as suddenly as it all began, it would end, leaving the world washed and scrubbed and greener than before, steaming spices from deep in the black soil, and topped with a rainbow. But afraid? Never. Somehow I knew Daddy would get us through anything that happened, and he always did.

Fall came. The aspens in the high lands turned golden and the willows took on the autumn maroon glow. We moved to town and I went to the strange new school. There were about 20 kids in the class, with most of whom I later graduated. They were kids a lot like me and accepted me quickly into their circle. In October and November, the Girl Scouts went after boughs of pine and Oregon Grape and with the help of lots of dedicated leaders made gorgeous Christmas wreaths to sell. The tradition still endures.

In December, the kids congregated on the ski hill, after school and on weekends. A chairlift season pass on Snow King Mountain cost $12.50. Skiing persisted, for many of us, as the number one pastime sometimes through April. And at the end of May, the Wogensens once again headed for the Gros Ventre.

June is the rainy month in Northwestern Wyoming, so quite often I would while away those wet cool hours with my feet propped on the oven door, drawing pictures of ladies with long wavy hair, huge shapely bosoms, and carefully hidden hands and feet. But as soon as the sun shone again, out I'd go to discover whatever may have been new in the high country.

There were more packtrips, more streams to be fished, and always new adventures to be part of. Among my projects that summer was the domesticating of Dusty. Not that he wasn't a fine animal to ride and a good racehorse in spite of his accumulating years, but once you got both your feet on the ground, he was nasty. Since I was six, I had been optimistic about his being my friend, but whenever he would see me coming, halter in hand, he would lay back his ears and chase me out of the pasture. If I wasn't quick, I'd get nipped on the backside going through the fence.

"You've got to show him who's boss," Daddy had told me for years. Well now that I was 12, it

was time to show him just that.

It wasn't easy. I'd ride him the 1/4 mile or so down to Tepee Creek, tie him to a high branch and go off for an hour. Chances are, by the time I'd get back he'd have gone home without the bridle or possibly *with* the branch. Somehow he could undo a knot, break a branch, or rub the headstall off quicker and easier than any other horse we had. But as my knots got stronger and my judgment keener, I could gradually depend on his being there, and mad enough to eat me alive! The second he'd see me coming, back would go the ears flat against his head, and he would wind his nose and switch his tail and stamp his feet like a kid in a tantrum. At first he would nip at me, but after I rapped his nose sharply with the blunt end of my fishing pole a few dozen times, he would go through the motions of biting and look as absolutely mean as he could, but he wouldn't ever again quite clench his teeth together, and at last, I knew I was the boss. I loved the horse and I've thought since that he loved me too, but that no self-respecting equine with a touch of Arabian running proud in his blood wants to have to obey the whims of a green kid. So he had to take a little of the green out of me before we could communicate on the same level. Which was only fair.

We took a Saturday trip to town about twice a month (providing there wasn't a raincloud in the sky) at which time we would stock up with groceries and Mother would enjoy the convenience of her wringer-washer that plugged into the wall. At Goosewing, she washed clothes on the board and ironed with hot-off-the-griddle flat-irons. On one particular trip to town she was met by two mothers of my school friends who told her "what a shame" they thought it was that that "poor little girl" had to be "way up there" without any friends "all summer long." This misguided concern went completely to waste on us, and became a family joke for years to come.

All too soon, the seasons shifted again; school started and we all got swept into the various activities for which Jackson is famous. That Christmas Daddy gave me a .22 rifle (which I still have) and the next summer, I added target practicing to my already full days. At 13 I was beginning to mature a little and was probably better company and help to my Dad (although he may not remember it quite that way). I know I couldn't have enjoyed a time any more. The summer I was fourteen, Daddy bought me a beautiful walnut piano which he trucked all the way up the Gros Ventre in the spring, and all the

Photo Courtesy of A.K. Wogensen

way down to Jackson the following fall. I had not had piano lessons but I had a good ear for music and that summer I played every three-chorded tune I had ever heard.

Those last two summers I really fell in love with the land. I knew a great deal of it intimately by that time, having walked or ridden around every hill, through every stand of timber, and fished every bend in the streams. I began to view it, not as just a playground, but as a precious heritage—something to protect and preserve. A lot of living has passed between me and those cherished growing-up years, a lot of people and events have woven through my life, but those four short summers at the Goosewing Ranger Station in the Tetons did more to shape the character of the woman I was to be than any other time since.

There was a legend in my childhood—the great Speas Spring. My Daddy spoke of it in hushed tones. He considered it one of the most valuable assets in Natrona County, He spoke of it as other men speak of a mosque or a cathedral, a place of beauty and wonder where miracles occur.

Having returned from the New Mexico desert, where I lived in a town that depended on the great mountain springs, I can more fully appreciate Daddy's attitude. On our Great American Desert, a spring means life.

To Daddy the spring meant the possibility of having a ranch with irrigated hay meadows and an

The Speas Spring

Helen Fisher Schmill
Casper

Photo Courtesy of the
Wyoming Game & Fish Commission

apple orchard instead of cactus-covered flats laced with the bones of dinosaurs, a place for cattle and a chance of college educations for the children. A spring offered the hope of civilization to a wild frontier and a family heritage. A man's soul as well as his fortunes could be bound up with a permanent spring.

The Speas spring, now the proud possessor of a hatchery division of the Wyoming Game and Fish Commission, continues to bless the state, just as Daddy knew it would. Its abundant cold waters prepare the young trout for life in the high country streams of Wyoming. Its goodness radiates into the peace of mind of contented fishermen who are better family men for catching trout that come from the Speas Fish Hatchery.

The buffalo and the Indians who watered at the Speas spring are all gone now. The old apple orchards are lost to decay. But the spring persists, as alive as ever, living up to its name as one of the hopes as well as one of the miracles of the West. The mountain snowmelt that percolates through the ground to emerge at the spring still brings life from Heaven to that sacred place, making the spring almost the maternal thing.

No one can stand in the presence of a big spring, watching the waters pour out, and not sense something of the deep and silent mysteries of the Earth. To contemplate a spring is to experience a little of the feeling of eternity. Geology becomes more than a book of theories. The rocks bear life, the life of the water that permits the life of plant and animal forms—and we ourselves—to flourish around the spring.

The Speas spring flows ten million gallons of water daily, at a constant temperature of sixty degrees the year around. It was covered by Territorial water right dated 1888. The sweet water, which has served the fish hatchery since 1958, also irrigates 700 acres of hay. It is the biggest fresh water spring in the state at a single hole, the hole being a half-acre in size. The water comes from the Tensleep formation.

We do well to maintain respect like my father's for this spring. It is a place to wonder and worship Him who made it and keeps it flowing.

Photo Courtesy of the
Wyoming Game & Fish Commission

Cinquains

*Mary Paine
Sheridan*

Impact

No one
kept it secret.
People go where work is.
Anyway a person has to live.
But how?

Wyoming Evening

Cattle
pepper evening.
Sprinkling a thousand hills
before the over easy sun
goes down.

Confession

Mountain
meadows weeping
sky blue forget-me-nots,
do penance for the tardiness
of Spring.

The Windmill

Lester Merha
Sheridan

Pete Nolan yawned and scratched his shaggy gray head. His arthritic limbs refused to respond immediately when he rose off the bed. His ears attuned to listen to any unusual sound outside, Pete glanced out the east window. No familiar creaking sound came from the windmill. He scowled, suddenly remembering that the windmill was broken.

Old Shep bounced off the porch and barked as if he meant business. Pete cocked his good ear toward the front yard. He recognized the sound of tires scrabbling over red shale. Somebody was coming up the lane to his ranch. Pete scowled again and reached for his pants.

"Damn it. When are they goin' to stop pesterin' me." He pushed his feet into a pair of slippers and buttoned his shirt, sticking the tail into his pants as he headed for the back door.

Sheriff Dunlop came through the yard gate and spoke to Shep. The dog stopped growling when Pete spoke to him. The sheriff stopped short of the porch and rocked back on his high-heeled boots.

"Good morning, Pete. Did you see anybody snooping around your place in the last twenty-four hours?"

"Not that I know of. I'd a run the bastard off if I'd seen him. More trouble at the mine?"

Dunlop's brows arched in surprise. "You've already heard about it?"

"Heard about what?"

"That the main office at the mine was busted into last night. They got away with Harrigan's radio and camera after breaking open the pop machine."

Pete's heavy brows formed a wide V. He looked beyond Dunlop. Along the road in front of his place all types of vehicles were kicking up dust. It was the time of day when the shifts changed at the mine.

"If Harrigan keeps hirin' all them long-haired, whiskered pilgrims from out-a-state, he better keep ever'thing nailed down tight. Anybody see who did it?"

"The nightwatchman saw two suspicious looking characters. He only got a good look at one of 'em, who was runnin' like hell. He had long hair and a pack on his back. The pack was orange color. Well, if you see any transients—strangers to you—let me know, Pete."

"How can I let you know? I don't have a phone."

Dunlop paused on his way back to the black and white sedan. "Say, that's right. Why don't you tell Bob Fisher when he comes by with the mail."

Pete didn't say anything while he watched the sheriff get into his car and drive off. Out of habit he tipped his head in a listening attitude, expecting to hear the squeaking complaint of the pump rod on the windmill. All he heard was the Wyoming wind whistling around the steel rods that braced the tower. Now that Dunlop had mentioned Bob Fisher coming by with the mail, Pete remembered the parts he had ordered for the windmill and figured this might be the day he'd get them.

He turned into the kitchen and stoked the stove with pine wood for a quick fire and sat down in a straight-backed chair to pull on his boots. Taking a wash basin over to the galvanized metal sink, Pete coaxed water from the hand pump. For the last forty years he had lived as a bachelor without modern conveniences of any kind.

The blissful solitude he had enjoyed all those years had skidded to an abrupt end. All around his 160-acre ranch, mining equipment was gouging the land for coal. Land speculators, realtors, and industrialists continued to beat a path to his door, wanting him to sell out. Tired of their interrupting visits, he'd painted a crude sign and fastened it on the gate facing the road.

KEEP OUT. ANYBODY CAUGHT TRESPASIN WILL BE PERSECUTED TO THE FULL EXTENT OF ONE MUNGREL DOG AND A DUBLE BARREL SHOTGUN THAT AIN'T LOADED WITH CUSHIONS.

Pete hardly had his breakfast things put away when old Shep started raising a ruckus down by the corrals in back of the barn.

He knew by the way the dog barked, it was worth investigating. Old Shep had something or somebody cornered.

Breaking the breech on his shotgun, he inserted two shells loaded with BBshot. He slapped on his hat and stepped outside. The dog was still barking, but he sounded closer to the windmill. Pete passed through the back yard gate before he saw the young man.

The lanky fellow had long hair the color of wheat straw and a scraggly beard. His shirt and pants were of faded denim and he had a packsack on his back. He stood looking at the windmill, his legs spread wide and his arms held akimbo. Encouraged by Pete's approach, Shep showed his fangs and was ready to grab one of the young stranger's legs.

Pete raised his shotgun to a threatening position. "What you doin' on my property?"

A glint of fear came into the young man's blue eyes when he stared at the Greener held in Pete's horny hands. "I just wanted to take a look at your windmill, sir. Why isn't it working?"

"The damn thing's busted, that's why it ain't workin'."

The kid gave him a half smile when Pete lowered his shotgun. Oddly, the young fellow reminded him of an aggressive pup eager to play.

"Do you know what's broken, sir?"

"Sure, I know what's busted. I got the parts ordered, but they must be sendin' 'em by the way of Siberia. Why're you so all-fired interested in a busted windmill?"

The youth grinned. "Man, I just can't see a windmill standing idle from neglect. It's like abandoning an elevator full of grain.''

Pete turned skeptical. He looked beyond the youth, to the right and the left of him. He glanced back over his own shoulder.

''You tryin' to trick me, young'n? Where's your pardner?''

''What partner?''

Pete eyed the young man's long hair and the pack on his back. ''Why the night watchman at the mine seed you and another kid sneakin' round the office. It was busted into last night.''

The young stranger quickly lost his composure when he saw Pete raise the shotgun in line with his belt buckle.

''Look man, I had nothing to do with it. I got away from there fast when some weirdo gave me a line about the office staying open all night, that we should hit up the mine foreman for a job. I knew he was trying to suck me into something.

''I reckon the night watchman was right. He did see you, didn't he?''

The youth's eyes grew wider. ''How did you find out? Look, I'll admit the guy did see me, but not until I'd parted company with that jerk. I didn't want to hang around and answer a lot of stupid questions, so I took off. Honest. That's the truth.''

Pete's arms ached from holding up the heavy shotgun. He lowered it again. ''Do you know the sheriff's lookin' for you?''

''No, sir.'' The youth glanced up at the windmill again. ''Could I climb up to the top of the windmill and see what's broken?''

Pete lifted the gun to a higher angle. ''So you can warn your pardner ? Not on your life.''

The youth slowly removed his packsack and dropped it in front of Pete. ''You can look through my pack. You won't find anything stolen in it.''

''Maybe you cached the stuff. How do I know?''

The young man shrugged. He studied Pete for a moment before pivoting and striding toward the windmill. ''Go ahead, shoot me if you want. I'm going to see what's wrong with your windmill.''

With the agility of a monkey the long-legged kid scampered up the ladder on the side of the tower and examined the spider and mechanism on the windmill. He didn't gaze at the rolling hills, but concentrated on the working parts, his fingers exploring each cam, sprocket and gear. He shouted down to Pete.

''Can you hand me some wrenches?''

''You can come down and fetch 'em yourself. I sure ain't packin' any up to you.''

When the young stranger reached the ground,

Pete escorted him into a log building with a sod roof. The shop area was in order with every tool in its proper place. The kid searched intently through a pile of iron heaped in one corner that Pete had accumulated through the years.

''You won't find anything to fix a windmill in that junk.''

The youth gave him a disarming smile as he removed an old pump from the pile. He lugged it over to the work bench and removed one of the drive shafts. He worked as though he knew what he was doing.

Soon Pete forgot about the possible danger of the kid turning on him. He leaned the shotgun against the outside wall of the shop. The kid scrambled back up to the platform at the top of the tower and within a few minutes replaced the broken drive shaft with the one he had removed from the old pump. Then he asked Pete to release the brake holding the windmill stationary.

Pete pushed the handle fastened to a guy wire serving as a brake to turn on, or shut off, the windmill. The wind pushed the rudder around so fast the young man had to duck this head. The wheel spun with dazzling speed in the sunlight. Once more Pete heard the squeaking, musical sound of the pump rod working up and down. He couldn't restrain himself.

''Hooray! Come on down, son.''

While waiting for the youth to descend the tower, Pete heard rubber screech on the road just beyond the gate. A cloud of red dust boiled around the braked car. Halfway down the ladder the kid paused to watch the vehicle barrel its way down the lane. The driver hadn't stopped to close the gate after passing through. A decal, bearing the bright letters of the REED MINING COMPANY, was plastered on each side of the two-door sedan. Harrigan, the company's manager, was behind the wheel.

The kid had reached the ground by the time the car came to a bouncing stop. He didn't turn to flee when Harrigan jumped out and yelled at him.

''Hey, you! Don't you run away. I want to talk to you.'' Harrigan sprinted toward the youth who had made no move to run.

Pete backed toward the workshop and picked up his shotgun, ''Hold it!''

Harrigan stopped suddenly as if yanked backward by an invisible rope. He had seen Pete make his move toward the scattergun and thought the old man looked as ringy as a Brahma bull on the prod. Harrigan pointed an accusing finger at the kid's packsack lying on the ground and then at the kid.

"That's him! He's one of 'em. Didn't the sheriff tell you this guy had an orange-colored packsack? That scrawny bastard stole my land camera and radio. They cost me over three-hundred bucks."

"How you know he did?" Pete asked. "You got proof?"

"Why yes, my night watchman described him for me."

"One thing I know about you, Harrigan. You don't believe in signs and you don't close gates."

"Oh, I'm sorry about not closing the gate, Mr. Nolan. I was so intent on preventing this thief from escaping I couldn't let one second slip by for fear the creep would get away. I hope you understand."

"Well, I don't, you dumb jehu, and closing a gate is just as important to me as your precious time. You got no right to rip the guts out of the earth God intended for animals to graze on. The oil company that owns the mine you operate wants to buy me out. Well, they ain't gettin' one handful of dust off my land. And if you ever want to get back on it, you'd better ask me first; savvy? Now, turn your butt around and get the hell out of here."

Harrigan stared at the finger resting on one of the triggers of the shotgun. He didn't trust the gleam in the old man's eyes or the way his hands trembled. Quickly he slid behind the wheel and backed the sedan all the way to the road.

The kid walked over to where Pete stood. "Mr. Nolan, I'm sorry I caused you so much trouble, but thanks a lot. I hope your windmill runs a long time."

Pete lowered the shotgun and searched the young man's face. Now that he looked beyond the kid's long wavy hair and his scraggly whiskers, he saw a person with guts and pride in what he did.

"Now don't go galivantin' off. I want to know why you was so determined to fix my windmill."

The kid adjusted the straps on the packsack and shrugged his slim shoulders. "Maybe I don't like what that joker from the mine represents any more than you do. Anyway, I got a thing about windmills. They're a kind of symbol of freedom to me—a freedom everybody enjoyed before material gain became their prime motive."

Pete extracted the shells from the Greener. "O.K., I believe you. Let's shoot the breeze over a cup of coffee." He pivoted quickly when he heard another car coming down the lane. "Now, who in—? Oh, it's Bob Fisher. He must have some mail for me."

The mail carrier patiently waited for Pete to put his shotgun aside and shuffle up to the station wagon. He leaned out of the open window and handed Pete a large package.

"Your parts for the windmill finally showed up, Pete. Why don't you put in an electric pump instead of—Hey! The windmill's running!"

Fisher looked at Pete and then at the young man. Pete and the kid exchanged knowing glances. Fisher pressed on the accelerator, as if intending to turn the station wagon back toward the road, but hesitated when he gave the kid another look.

"Oh, I nearly forgot, Pete. Sheriff Dunop told me to tell you that he caught the punk who broke into Harrigan's office last night."

Pete thanked the mail carrier and winked at the kid who grinned. He put his hand on the younger man's shoulder as they walked toward the house. "Sure good to hear that old windmill creaking away—free as the wind that turns it."

Someone Left Summer

Peggy Simson Curry
Casper

Someone left summer by the roadside
  In a bale of hay.
It was winter when we passed it by,
  Driving the car
Among wind-tumbled February hills,
  And down all down that day
I held the mountain meadows close
  Sun—rain—the sunflowers hours
Blown warm, moon-turned in arms of trees.

What shall we have when love is chaff,
  Our fields fallow with frost?
Grant some small highway of the heart
  By bundled grass or grain
Be marked in all our snowy traveling
  That we may smile and say,
''Ah, what a summering was there!''

Photo Courtesy of Midge Swartz

Our Beautiful-Ugly Christmas Bird

Midge Swartz
Gillette

A wild turkey. I had never seen one, but I knew at once what it was. Well, almost at once.

"Ed, look," I yelled at my husband as I clawed at the door of our moving pick-up. "It's a vulture. It's got to be. Stop. It's so big and black. Stop!"

I immediately disqualified the idea. After all, our cattle ranch is in northeastern Wyoming, and we had just been out cutting our Christmas tree.

It was a warm day considering that for the last two weeks the temperature had stayed steadily between thirty and forty degrees below zero. But even so, it was cold, and my mind's trivia file linked vulture with deserts and heat.

Ed finally stopped the vehicle. He muttered as we jumped out, just a few yards short of the garage, and looked into the shelter belt.

There it was. A long-legged, long-necked, big-bodied bird showing black against the snow.

"I'll be damned. A wild turkey!" he said as the bird scurried back through the trees and disappeared.

Turkeys are so rare in our country that a small flock of three or four had been seen just once way up north on our place. I knew my father-in-law journeyed often to the Black Hills country to hunt them and came home empty-handed due to the scarcity of the bird. So I was enamored with the sight and with the thought that I had seen a turkey almost in my very own yard.

The turkey stayed but was quite shy, so we did a lot of sneaking around to watch. We decided that it was a hen, that she had fallen in with a flock of pheasants we feed each winter, and that, evidently, when the cold spell hit, the pheasants brought her along to food and survival.

She was still with us on Christmas day. It seemed only right that she be there to add to our rural greeting card scene of deer and antelope, pheasants and partridge feeding near the house. We had expected her to be gone by then, and we joked about having a turkey for Christmas that was still walking around.

Winter progressed. The snow from November stayed on until March, and the birds were in the north shelter belt all day long feeding from the grain boxes.

Then came the day I looked out my kitchen window to the south and saw that the turkey had joined the pheasants at the boxes Ed had moved as a lure to a spot we could watch from indoors. She was nervous at first being so close to the house, but she soon felt at ease. I do not really remember naming her, but in my mind she had been Turkey Lurkey from the start. We watched her every chance we got, and she was a living nature lesson just as all the wild things are on the ranch.

She was a big bird and seemed ugly at first glance with her lump of a body, big feet, long legs, skinny neck, little bare head and beady eyes. But we found that her darkish brown feathers had a sheen of copper in the sunlight. Her wing and tail feathers were speckled or banded with white and black, and she walked with her tail pointing directly at the ground.

She was about thirty inches tall, and she usually walked slowly and gracefully, head bobbing a bit with each step. It was her head that was so amazing.

All feathers stopped about halfway up her neck except for a sparse row which went up the back to her head. The only other growth was a few whisps of what looked like baby hair on the bare front part of the neck.

Mr. Turkey must have gotten the flashy looks for the family, but our Ms. Turkey had one splash of glory with pink and blue skin on her neck and blue skin on her head from the beak to behind her shiny eyes. She had a wattle, but it was just a small flap of skin which followed the contour of her neck so closely that it was seldom noticeable. The finishing touch was between her nose and eyes where a couple of very coarse feathers grew up and forward, looking much like a unicorn's horn. She was really something else when it was all put together.

The ranch cats stalked Turkey Lurkey quite a bit a first. They would hide behind something, forgetting their giveaway tails twitching in the air above them and in plain sight of their prey. She was very polite and simply walked far around, pretending she did not notice. I have never figured out what any cat thought he would do if he caught that full-grown turkey, and I do not think the cats thought of it before-hand either. Luckily for them they never had to find out.

The snow melted, the days warmed, and still she stayed with us. Now she ventured into the yard, and after a few whippings and many harsh words, the dogs left her alone. When frightened, she would fly beautifully to a perch on the roof or in a tree, and then she would just gobble like the devil at whatever had scared her. Her favorite perch was on the top of a big cottonwood tree. The branch she chose always seemed too frail, but there she would sit, balancing constantly with wings and tail whenever the wind blew.

I would talk to Turkey Lurkey whenever I was outside and throw her popcorn and then shake the jar. Soon the noise of the rattling corn would bring her from wherever she was, and I could make her come closer each time before I would feed her. It was not long until she would let any of us touch her, as a prelude to getting to the corn of course. We were amazed that after months of being frightened, she became tame so fast.

The talk of all our neighbors was the turkey. People got such a kick out of seeing her walking around the place, undisturbed by kids, dogs, cattle or vehicles, and quite curious about anything different.

One day she watched us wash the car. She came closer and closer, cocking her head to watch the water dripping and trying to peck the drops, and following us all around the car until she was a nuisance. Finally, seeming to be completely stumped as to what we were doing, she flew with great majesty to land on the clean hood with her huge muddy feet. Smoothing her feathers, she looked at us knowingly as though the new vantage point would make everything clear to her.

As it usually happens, we presumed too much and bought a hundred pound sack of corn toward the end of April. The next day, Turkey Lurkey was gone.

We talked about how she was just heeding the spring mating urge and had left to look for one of her own kin. We did not talk about our fears that some passer-by could not resist a turkey dinner placidly strolling so close to the road.

We miss that beautiful-ugly bird. We even miss her frightening, scolding gobble coming out of the night from her cottonwood tree perch when we would come home late from town and disturb her. But we always have to end our rememberances of her with one thought. How many people get the gift of a Christmas turkey that lasts until Easter?

Many people have heard the claim that the famed, honored Jackalope was first discovered by a trapper near Douglas, Wyoming, in 1829. It is said that mountain-men swapped yarns of the odd animal as they lolled around blazing campfires. Adventurer John Colter, the story goes, mentioned the Jackalope only to his closest friends.

However, few folks are familiar with the person who created its image in taxidermy and started it on the road to fame. Laying claim to this honor is Douglas Herrick, age 51, an ambitious man with a keen imagination and a home near Casper, Wyoming.

"Grandfather used to tell us tales of this great rare creature of the plains when we were kids," related Mr. Herrick. "Brother Ralph had shot a giant jackrabbit on a hunting trip near the town of Douglas, in the fall of 1941. The horns of a buck deer hung in the garage at home. He cut the small end horns off and screwed them on the big rabbit's head. It looked exactly like grandfather's description of a Jackalope.

Ray Ball, manager of the La Bonte Hotel in Douglas, Wyoming, bought the Jackalope from the Herrick brothers for ten dollars. As a direct result of vigorous advertising, the animal,

Photo Courtesy of John Bonar

John Bonar
Glenrock

How the Jackalope was Born

24

numbering into the thousands, has wandered its way into every state in the Union, including Alaska and Hawaii, and hopped its way across the ocean into far-way Iran and countries of Europe.

The Jackalope is known as one of the most unusual nature-freaks in the world. Its shape and coloring is like a rabbit, except that it has horns. It is too small to pass as a deer. Termed vicious when attacked, most other animals have great respect for the Jackalope's sharp set of prong horns. Herders singing the lonesome nights away claim to have heard their words repeated like an echo rebounding from the high hills. This echo they attribute to the Jackalope. It usually occurs, they say, on calm dark nights and always before a crashing thunderstorm. It is also told that hunting hounds have spun in their tracks trying to trace the lightning swift, horned rabbit streaking through the darkness at ninety miles an hour. Blending with the color of the countryside the animals are seldom seen during the daylight hours. A thirty-mile speed of a jackrabbit added to the fleet sixty-mile an hour take-off developed from its antelope ancestery stirs air friction aiding a good hunter to set his gun sights ahead of the flying target. Sharpshooters seldom have proof of a direct hit but many of them brag of near misses.

Varied are the traveler's visions of this fleet-footed oddity. An easterner remarked to her spouse as she spied a large jackrabbit—"There's one of those funny things without the horns."

Meanwhile Jackalope potatoes fill floor space at grocery marts. An inviting Warm Spring Jackalope Pool is located in Douglas, Wyoming. Entering town, a roadside sign with large letters warns "Watch out for Jackalope!" Enterprising merchants slip labels on small milk cans listing it as Jackalope Milk. Motel owners display one dollar license cards entitling the bearer to hunt Jackalope with the stipulation that a thousand dollar fine is in order if a hunter bags a two-tailed creature under any circumstances. Five out-of-state hunters spent a week in the nearby Chalk Buttes searching for the elusive beast, only come out exhausted and empty handed, although they said that rabbits having horn-like portrusions were evident.

"We saw many does, but no bucks...with the big horns," they sadly admitted.

Could it be that the now world famous Jackalope is a bit like Santa Claus? Although he is rarely seen, we know that he is around.

Photo Courtesy of Nancy Bradberry

Reprinted from *IN WYOMING*
Jan. Feb. 1974

Mythology About Wyoming

Mike Leon
Story

Photo Courtesy of Nancy Bradberry

Before we get carried away by a growing mythology about Wyoming, I think we ought to examine it critically.

That mythology insinuates that this State is an unsullied paradise whose ranching folk display an incomparable life style, where the environment has been painstakingly taken care of by them and where industry intrudes only to the detriment of the status quo.

It is true that Wyoming demonstrates certain unique qualities, although they are fading fast and not only because of industry but because of population growth and intensifying recreationist activity. A visitor from North Carolina recently observed to me that in all her travels she had seen nothing so "inviolate" as Wyoming, meaning Wyoming is relatively unscarred compared to the rest of the country. That much is obvious.

What is not so obvious is the Wyoming has been abused seriously from the very start, by overgrazing in particular; and its social history, beginning with the ruthlessness with which the region was seized from its original inhabitants, has been a dubious one. The casual observer does not know of the violence on the isolated ranches—only the circuit riding clergyman knows of that—or of the suicide, divorce and alcoholism statistics which suggest that "God's Country" is a troubled area indeed.

Where has the major opposition to setting aside Wilderness come from? Industry? Industry has been emphatic in its opposition but not so shrill as organized stockgrowers. Who were behind the attempts after World War II to have BLM land sold off to private interest for a song? I leave the answer to you. The point is this: Wyoming is and long has been a less-than ideal situation and the current mythology about its paradise-like qualities is, well, mythology.

Photo Courtesy of Nancy Bradberry

I advise those who disagree with me to study what the main issues were during the 1950's, 1960's and the first two years of the 1970's in rural Wyoming. They had nothing to do with protecting Wyoming environment, nothing to do with preserving and enhancing a life style which now, nostalgically, is discovered to be precious.

What am I getting at? Just this. If our opposition to industry is based on saving virginal Wyoming from a fate worse than death then I think industry can rightly be cynical about our motives or at least skeptical about our powers of observation. If we take the position that the only threat to Wyoming's environmental qualities is industry when we may rightly be accused of injustice.

The real Wyoming is unknown to a majority of its residents, and I doubt there are a handful of people around the nation who understand it. It is badly written about, not only by those adjective-prone reporters from various eastern and western publications—their favorites in describing Wyoming being "vast" and "empty"—but by its native sons and daughters who perpetuate the mythology because mythology is where the money is. Someday, perhaps, we will have the truth about Wyoming, the awful hungers over water and land, the real reasons behind the antagonism to the federal government, the sense of nature and climate as cruel and capricious enemies.

As for industry, it has a golden opportunity to be a positive force, if only it would embrace the challenge. Wyoming has an unrealized potential that makes today's mythology misleading and a burden.

Reprinted from the Sheridan Press
July 23, 1975

Photo Courtesy of Nancy Bradberry

Wyoming Hillsides

Lulu Goodrick
Fort Bridger

Sage stubbled cheeks
Wind wrinkled and marred,
Jaws unshaven
Rock pimpled and scarred.

Make the Green a *wild* River!

Otis Carney
Cora

Reprinted from NEW LEASE ON LIFE
by permission of author and
Random House Inc., publishers

At the age of forty-six, Otis Carney, successful script writer in Hollywood, quit the Big Game. He loaded his wife, Teddy, and three sons in a station way, drove away from a "lotusland" existence in Beverly Hills, California, and plowed into a snowbank known as Cora, Wyoming. The family plowed into the work of running a cattle ranch. Their experiences, satisfactions and traumas are recorded in Carney's book New Lease on Life.

The following is an excerpt from that book: [*The Carneys had gone back to California to sell their house.*]

Photo Courtesy of Elsa Spear Byron

"Tell me that again." I said on the phone. "They're going to do *what* to the Green River?"

"Make it a Wild River," my friend answered. He was calling from Wyoming, where he was involved in politics and water matters.

"What the hell does a Wild River mean?"

"Some headaches for you and other ranchers. In fact, it might even put you out of business."

"Ah, come on. How?"

"Because they want to condemn a strip of land a quarter of a mile wide on each side of the river, turn it over to the public."

"They can't do that! On all these ranches, the houses are in that strip. So are the ranch buildings, corrals, ditches..."

"Like I told you," he said, "it's serious. You'd better think about coming up here. This is going to be quite a fight."

A few days later I got a telegram from one of the Wyoming senators, asking me to appear as a witness at a Senate hearing on the Wild River proposal, to be held in the high school at Green River City. Then, in the mail, I received a preliminary Interior Department study on the Wild River, complete with maps. My heart sank. The strip of land to be condemned did indeed snake right through our ranch, following the river. It would cut the heart and guts out of the place. There was even a provision for a paved road running along the river near our house and slicing the ranch in two. If this wasn't enough, they'd add a site for an amusement park (on a Wild River?) just north of our heifer pasture.

Here we were trying to sell the place in Beverly Hills and move to the ranch and now Wyoming appeared to be going up in smoke. Exhaust, that is, and fisherman and hunters' cars, picnickers, shooters, looters. I knew one thing: even if they moved our buildings outside the public zone, it wouldn't be safe to stick your head outdoors. You might as well try homesteading in the Battle of the Bulge.

Neither Teddy nor I knew what to do. We'd had no experience with conservation and even less with Wyoming politics. But the reflex of a writer is to find out facts and then fight back with words. I got on the phone and called my neighbors. To these hardy ranchers in Wyoming, any intrusion by the government is suspect at best, and the reaction was practically unanimous. A majority of people in Sublette County were bitterly opposed to making the Green a Wild River. So was the governor, and the Wyoming delegation in Congress, with the exception of Senator Gale McGee. That seemed good enough for me. But

Photo Courtesy of Elsa Spear Byron

then, one rancher friend disagreed. "I ain't sure at all," he muttered, "whether we'd better not get in and take this Wild River. Fix up the wording so we can live with it. Because if we don't, I just got an idea that the state is going to turn around and dam us out."

"A dam?" I said.

"You bet. For forty years they've been talking about putting in this Kendall Dam, a few miles below your place. It would wipe you out and the whole valley with you."

"So it's kind of an either-or, but they get you both ways?"

"That's about what it comes to."

I wish now that I had listened to this man. For what he predicted came true. Only a handful realized it then, and the greater tragedy was that our stretch of river and valley became a hot potato tossed back and forth between the federal government and the state of Wyoming.

Actually, both sides, federal and state, had a plausible case. They just went at it wrong. In the Study Report on the Wild River, which is a noble idea, the Interior Department should have realized that each proposed Wild River had a different problem in terms of ownership of bank lands. For instance, some rivers in Idaho flow almost totally through already-public lands, federal or state-owned. There are a few pieces of private ground along the banks—mining claims, homesteads. Since these are usually abandoned, they can be condemned by the government with little hardship to the owners. To classify such a river as Wild means that you keep roads, dams, development, timbering, mining or motels out of it. I couln't agree more.

But here on the Green, it was obvious that old-timers had settled big ranches, grubbed hay meadows and made large investments in sweat and money, directly alongside the serpentine river. To ask these ranchers to give up their bank lands to the public was tantamount to asking a private homeowner to yield, say his four-foot entrance walk through his front yard, through his house and out the back. Give it over to the public, and then have the effrontery to tell the homeowner that he can still live and operate his business in his home.

Such a scheme was patently impossible, and every rancher up and down the Green knew it.

Moreover, they also knew that the public already had full access to float the river, fish it; the only prohibition was going up on the banks, on private land. Wyoming, with its landowner-dominated legislature, is very strict about trespass laws. As strict, say, as a factory owner would be if he didn't want the public wandering through his plant all day long.

But there was a solution, which I could see even then. Though it might take patient selling to some of these leathery, independent ranchers, I felt it could be done. A Wild River on the Green would prevent any dams, any future junky development or polluting industries that would destroy one of the last real wildernesses in the United States. Now, the rancher didn't want any of these things either. So my idea was: use the concept of the Wild River, not as a condemnation of bank lands, but as a zoning. The ranchers would agree to a zoning that would guarantee in perpetuity that their ranches would remain as they are at present, untouched by dams, roads, industry, etc. To be sure, I knew that the ranchers, with their natural suspicion of anything "government" would consider such zoning as an infringment. They worried about "Washington changing its mind, grabbing our land someplace down the road." But the risk seemed to me worth taking, for in the long run it might be the only way to preserve our lands for those who wanted to enjoy a truly wild river.

I wrote this recommendation into my testimony before the senators at the Green River High School. But I was already too late. War had been declared: Wyoming versus Washington. Tempers heated up; nobody listened to anyone else. No one tried to rewrite legislation, at least not in time to save the Green. Later, ironically, in the less passionate halls of Congress the Wild Rivers Act was amended to include what were called Scenic Rivers. In these, there was no condemnation of private bank lands. Instead, it was tantamount to a zoning, protecting the river as is, which was what many people had hoped for on the Green.

But, in the political pressure, we fell between two horses, and the Green was omitted from the bill. It wasn't too many months before the state of Wyoming would begin to plan exactly what my rancher friend had warned: build the Kendall Dam, wipe us out.

Postscript: The Kendall Dam was never built.

It seems an eternity since the first rumblings and rumors of sudden and drastic change began to filter through to this quiet place. In fact, it is less than five years.

In order to act in a positive way, it is important to be able to understand and evaluate the complicated issues and situations now facing those of us living in Wyoming, Montana, and indeed the West. This requires pulling together not only all of the education one has acquired in a formal sense and what life has taught, but also learning new skills and disciplines. Without such an approach it is easy to be overwhelmed by what is happening.

It almost goes without saying that the place where one grows up is a major governing factor in life. Both the positive and negative aspects of the place in which one spends childhood and formative years influence choices throughout the rest of a lifetime. What then does it mean to grow up on a ranch in Wyoming?

The only way to describe it is to be autobiographical. My childhood memories are of one long summer when I was free to climb onto the warm round back of my pony, provided always I could catch her, ride up into the aspen groves on the face of the mountain, and slip off for a while to play and drink from a clear mountain brook. Now

Carolyn Wallop Alderson
Big Horn, WY
Birney, MT

A Place to Live

and then I would cross over to an island in the creek that ran by our house and play "pioneer," or squat for hours in the water, picking up the shining multi-colored rocks. I'd place them carefully on the bank only to find that as they dried they always turned gray. The only way to preserve the color was to return them to the water. At the time it was a frustrating lesson; now I watch as nature teaches it to my own children.

Sometimes I would ride my pony in the hay fields. As I urged her over the bales I would suddenly be transported to Madison Square Garden, winning all the blue ribbons at the National Horse Show. The giant boulders in Little Goose Canyon made excellent castles within which I could be an enchanted princess; and there were empty houses around, definitely haunted. In the late summer and fall I would fill my little wagon with sour red crabapples and pull them around—eating some, though I gathered them only because they were pretty. I spent a lot of time lying on my back in the golden grass looking at clouds, watching the cottonwoods shimmer and talking to my collie. Winter memories consist of school, making snow forts and sledding down what seemed like very fast dangerous hills.

The place, with its hideouts and secrets, and my imagination were my friends. Time and my elders' apparent control of it, my enemies. I wasn't aware then that I 'loved' the place; my feelings were not contained in a word. In fact, I am sure that I took the entire time and experience for granted. Irresponsible? Perhaps. Except that I always had what seemed like endless chores and responsibilities. They came under the heading of my elder's control of time.

I frequently heard the phrase, "Clean your plate! Think of all the starving children in the world." But the phrase meant nothing to me, nor could I visualise what poverty and misery were because no one I knew was really poor. None of my school friends were without coats or food or warm houses. Some wore hand-me-downs, but then so did I and that was no disgrace. Naturally, there were degrees up and down the scale of having more or less, but it was not until I went East that I saw destitution. The grime and the gray green air of Baltimore, people standing aimlessly on street corners or staring vacantly out of broken windows depressed me terribly. It did not occur to me until very recently that there was not real poverty in Wyoming because it was essentially an agricultural community.

The contrast between poverty and affluence was uncomfortable for me at fourteen. The discomfort increases as I have come to understand that the reasons for both the contrast and the poverty is what is commonly called "progress." Wherever it takes place, industrialization first removes some agricultural land from production and its workers. And whether it is shipbuilding, or steel, coal, power plants, or copper, the wealth generated in an area seldom stays where it is produced. The Appalachian region of this country is the area richest of all in natural resources, and yet the word "Appalachia" is synonymous with poverty. Unless it can be proven that there is absolutely no alternative, this should not happen to Wyoming or the West.

Before I went away to school, and off and on after that, as I grew older, there were times, especially during winters, when I longed to find some action, different thinking, to meet other people who did other things. Cows and weather seemed to be all people talked about at home. At those times I thought that living on a ranch would be the dullest possible existence. I'm not sure when the realization that it would be impossible for me to live in a city or a suburb, and the recognition that the ranching business is indeed interesting, came together in my mind. It was some time before I finished college, but I did finish college and even tried to live in New York City. I was surprised to find that while I had interesting friends in the city, endless cultural opportunities and went to the "country" on weekends, I still felt hemmed in, with a curious mixture of irritation at the lack of privacy and a feeling that no one gave a damn what happened to me.

The more it bothered me, the more I realized that I was not accomplishing much there, so I sublet my apartment and came back to Wyoming. Another reason for this move could have been a letter I received from an extremely rational, down-to-earth cowboy which said: "I can understand being in New York in the winter but how can you stay there in the springtime?" He proceeded to describe the spring activities of beaver, cattle, trees and flowers. I never left after that, except to visit.

I later married that cowboy and am still learning from him of the endless allure of this country, and that the consequences of any given action toward the land have to be carefully weighed. Its ever changing beauty is easy to appreciate and many do, but the real fascination is in learning how to live within its perimeters and still make a living from it.

There were seven years of learning and growing things—babies, vegetables, cows, puppies. We were productive and molding a lifestyle. It all seemed secure and safe, and the future was fairly predictable—the same, more or less, as the past.

Then, in 1970, an amateur archaeologist came to the house to ask if we could identify arrowhead sites or tepee rings in the area. He told us that there were big plans for developing the coal reserves out here and that it would start to happen within five years. Soon, neighbors began to speak happily of leasing their coal for $2.00 an acre! This was more than oil leases brought and the oil had never been developed, so it would mean more free money. The cattle market was bad, so what could be better?

We were aware even then that leasing coal is quite a different matter from leasing oil. Soon there were ominous signs all around us that our archaeologist friend had not been wrong.

During the period, the spring and summer of 1971, the story of a woman I had known while I was in the East kept coming back to me. Its persistence filled me with anxiety. Lizel Wittenberg grew up in Vienna, the daughter of a Jewish textile manufacturer. She led a secure and happy childhood and eventually, with her parent's blessings, married a young lawyer, definitely on his way up. They had a son around 1937. For a long time the gathering clouds of Hitler's power didn't touch them. Then, very suddenly one night they were forced to flee with only the clothes on their backs and their child, to England. They spoke no English, which increased their isolation, and Lizel never saw her parents again.

Later they emigrated to this country and I knew the son as a medical school graduate. One day when I was visiting their house, I showed Lizel some photographs of our ranch in Wyoming.

"What lovely lovely pictures of the Alps!" she said.

"Lizel," I replied, "those aren't the Alps. They are the Big Horn Mountains in Wyoming."

She refused to believe me. The awesome realization came over me that life for her had stopped the moment she left Austria in 1940. Everything after that had merely been existence. She managed well enough, but life did not extend beyond her husband and son.

Lizel's story crowded my thoughts because I too have always been as secure as have most other white Americans. Lately the realization has come to me that there are forces at work even in our own country that, under the patriotic banner of Project Independence for the higher social and economic good of other parts of the country, can be just as destructive toward the people of the Northern Great Plains as Hitler's cry to "Make the world safe for Aryans!" was for an unwanted minority in Europe.

Every day now there was something in the newspapers about ranchers being threatened with condemnation for coal, or plans for mines, or clips about industrial water claims. One day we went to Billings, Montana, to a meeting we had been urged to attend. Normally we were not 'meeting goers.' The announcement of the gargantuan plan for developing Northern Plains coal came at that meeting. It was called the North Central Power Study. It outlined mine sites, railroad and aquaduct sites, and 42 different power plant sites. The same plan with variations exists now but it has no title because it soon became obvious to developers that the power study was an effective organizing tool!

All of this was to take place betwen Colstrip, Montana and Gillette and Buffalo, Wyoming in a sort of giant oval. With the announcement of the plan came industry propaganda too. There was an endless series of slide shows all over the area. The pictures were of blonde-haired young girls romping blythely in waist high grass and little boys and their fathers pulling splendid fish out of ponds. This, we were told, was what reclamation of mined land would do for our "dry useless land."

We weren't accustomed to taking someone's word for the gospel truth on outside issues before, so it was not unnatural to question these people, who in fact, were threatening everything we were and had.

Questions immediately came to us: Is it really necessary? Some of it? Any of it? And if it should turn out not to be necessary, except for balance sheets in corporate boardrooms, then what of the American system of government with its guaranteed civil and property rights? Would these rights protect us?

The important thing then became for us to gather all the information about energy, coal, strip mining, industrialization that we could, in order to be able to answer that question: Is it really necessary?

Our evaluation was accompanied by the background drumbeat of catch phrases like "free enterprise" and "patriotism," words symbolic of solid values. The demagogues in industry and government who use them also label the ranchers and farmers trying to save their lands as "environmentalists." This has become a catchword to imply that such people have no economic stake in what is happening, and therefore are not qualified to speak.

We were told that the "environmentalists" themselves had made western coal attractive and necessary because it was the only low-sulphur, and therefore clean, coal in the country. We were told that strip mining is the only economical way to extract coal because deep mining is both dangerous and labor expensive. It was also argued that we have only a few year's supply of petroleum and natural gas remaining, but that we have five hundred years of coal left. So the only way is to develop synthetic fuels as well as vast reserves of oil shale. Above all, it was impressed firmly upon us that the Middle East is a dangerous place to have to rely upon for energy, and that it is our patriotic duty to move to supply the nation the energy it needs.

As we organized ourselves into citizen groups such as the Nothern Plains Resource Council and the Powder River Resource Council, we also found friends and knowledgeable people in other parts of the country. Our information network was working well and we began to discover the truth about the sudden interest in western coal. We also discovered why the industrialization of the West is not only unnecessary but in fact economically bad for the rest of the country.

Strip mining is lucrative for the companies doing it, but it serves to keep deep mines dangerous, because corners are cut in their health and safety codes in order to remain competitive with strip mines. With all the worry of unemployment it is interesting to note that strip mines actually put deep miners out of work, particularly in the eastern coalfields. Perhaps, though, the worst thing about strip mining is that only a fraction of the total recoverable coal reserves is strippable—only about three to eighteen per cent depending upon definitions of "strippable."

It is a known fact that there are large reserves of coal elsewhere in the country. Illinois, for example, has the largest reserves of any single state in the union, and it is near large bodies of water and established labor pools—both necessary for developing synthetic fuel facilities.

It is true that some of the eastern coal is higher in sulphur, but it is also better quality by and large. It is often necessary to burn almost two tons of western coal to get the equivalent amount of heat, and western coal is very high in moisture content—from 24% to 40%. The net result is that the sulphur content of western coal is often as high or higher than the eastern coals.

We discovered that the real reason for the push to develop western coal is because it is owned in large blocks by the railroads and the Federal government. The fact that western coal is low in sulphur has less to do with the interest in it than the difficulties multinational companies would have acquiring similar amounts of eastern and midwestern reserves which are owned by many different entities. Federal leases can be acquired for very little money and held for a long time for speculative and collateral purposes.

It is said that we have five hundred years of coal left to use. That is according to present production of 600 million tons per year. If coal production is doubled, then the reserves are, of course, reduced by half. If exponential energy growth continues, and no one speaks of leveling off except "environmentalists," then the reserves shrink again.

If the Ford Administration's Project Independence should go through, energy will probably be so expensive that we would have to level off by painful necessity. A great deal of capital, both public and private, would be drained off by synthetic fuel production. Project Independence not only entails 100 billion dollars in direct subsidies and a Federal Energy Corporation similar to the Tennessee Valley Authority, but it also calls for price supports on all fuels to keep the illusion that synthetic fuels are competitive.

Officials in Wyoming and other western states are still laboring under the illusion that it is impossible to control development once it begins. The lessons of Colstrip power plants One, Two, Three and Four, with Five, Six and Seven planned, and of Rock Springs don't seem to be sinking in. Energy attracts energy intensive industries. There are, for example, rumors already of one, and possibly two aluminum processing plants that would use electricity from the plant that Basin Electric wants to build near Wheatland.

When these plants are built the population explodes in the location. The companies building them don't construct the roads or the schools or the hospitals. Federal, state and local taxpayers do. The human debris that is left for state social services to deal with is chalked up as a necessary part of "progress." Ranchers leasing or selling their surface over Federal coal are told that they will be able to use their ranches again after mining. Generally when a rancher is told something he assumes that the word of the person giving the information is good and that he is getting the truth.

The past is an integral part of ranching communities as is the idea of the continuity of the family on the land. The living awareness of history from the family and the community to the national level is not a 'Freedom Train' carrying Larry Mahan's rodeo championship belt buckle and other assorted trivia. It is found in people who have roots and a sense of responsibility to more than today.

The values of roots and family and history will be summarily wiped out if industrialization takes over the West. They will be wiped out by people who will come like locusts, unwittingly destroying small agrarian towns in their path. And those who know only ranching, farming and the land will try to move elsewhere, though 'elsewhere' will become impossible to find.

The conflict between the growth ethic and agriculture is rapidly coming to an apex in the nation. Whether the issue is deep water super-tanker ports in important fishing bays, taking irrigation water out of rivers for industry, strip mining, ruining forage crops with air pollution, or covering up farm land with towns, the final result is always decreased agricultural capacity.

The end result will be a food crisis in this country unless it is recognized that the time for leveling off is past due.

It is possible to level off. There is an enormous amount of waste and there are many alternatives to fossil fuels, such as sun and wind. It is possible to prevent this destruction of people and land. There is an interesting quote from the Bible:

"If the spirit of the ruler shall rise up against thee, leave not thy place, for yielding pacifieth great offenses."

Ecclesiasates, Chapter 10

The new frontiers of America should be in the areas of human awareness. Wyoming and the West can show the rest of the nation the road to that frontier. People living harmoniously with the land know that its secrets are only revealed slowly and quietly. The outrageous joy of watching a bean plant force its way out of the ground towards the sun to eventually give food is a gift no snowmobile or movie house can match. It is good to sit by a clear mountain stream and know that it will eventually flow on to an alfalfa field and back into a river to nurture fish for someone to catch. Preferable to thinking of the same water going into a huge pipe to be consumed in a gasification plant.

The coal has been here for 60 million years. We don't have to use it all up now. Let's leave some of it to nature's own good development.

If we could use the sun for power, it will still shine just as brightly a thousand years from now. If we harnesss the wind we will never tap its source. There are alternatives to raping the earth beneath us, thoughtlessly.

We should know that what we have in Wyoming is contributing to the nation. We should remain in our places and not yield for the short term gain. If we stand firm, or children and our great great grandchildren may yet keep this as the land they love. And the nation, too, will thank us for it.

Dilemma

Judy Skalla
Omaha, Neb

Mine!

The homeplace?

Brothers disagree.

Strip the fields our father plowed?

Fields that broke his heart can yield a crop!

Judy Skalla

Kleenburn, A Reclaimed Camp

Barbara Ketcham
Sheridan

Photo Courtesy of Dave Graunke

Kleenburn Camp with its verdant grass, myriad trees, and swimming and fishing ponds now resembles other Boy Scout camps in Wyoming. Twenty years ago, it was the site of a strip mining operation.

Located seven miles north of Sheridan, the newly formed Scout camp is an example of land reclaimed. Even its name, "Kleenburn" is from an old mining town in the same location.

Strip mining in the early 50's left two pits in the area.   One pit had been mined and was approximately eighty feet deep.   The second, thirty-five feet deep had the overburden removed but had never been mined. Today, both pits, stocked with fish, serve as canoe ponds as well as fishing holes. Various kinds of vegetation have taken over during the past twenty years, resulting in an abundance of flowers and other plants.

Besides its reclamation history, Kleenburn Boy Scout Camp is an example of cooperation and community spirit that still lives in Wyoming.

In 1969, several years after the mining operation closed, the hundred acres were given to Sheridan County and earmarked for recreation land but nothing more was done with it until 1973. Because the closest summer camp for Sheridan area Boy Scouts was the Buffalo Bill Camp in Cody, officials began checking possibilities for a camp site nearby. They investigated two pieces of land owned by the county and chose the Kleenburn site because of its accessibility.

Meetings with the County Commissioners and the County Recreation Board followed, finally yielding a fifty-year lease with Central Wyoming Boy Scout Council for the sum of $1 per year and the right to renew.

Terms of the lease? Only one—to have a working plan of improvements drawn up and approved by the County Recreation Board. A Scout leader and member of the Soil Conservation Service enlisted the help of his colleagues to draw up an over-lay map showing location of access roads, trees and brush locations, and accessiblity to water. From this, the development committee (made up of Scout leaders) was able to specify planned improvements such as site of picnic and parking areas, location of outdoor toilets, tables and water wells.

With the approval of the Recreation Board and County Commissioners, Garey Ketcham and other Scout leaders began to work on the land.

"It was a labor of love," said one leader describing the camp and how it was transformed from a scarred wilderness into a pleasant and useful area for Boy Scouts and others.

With $60 cash donations, the development committee not only found other willing hands, but many businessmen who are glad to donate their equipment, their men, and needed supplies.

If donations of labor were priced at the going rates, it is estimated that the total cost of Kleenburn Camp would be well over $10,000.

Bulldozers, graders, loaders, and trucks became familiar sights at the camp site as county and city road crews, heavy equipment operators from a construction company, and Army Reserve men volunteered their time.

It took several weeks to push the overburden down into the pond to eliminate a dangerously high bank along one of the ponds. Sheridan City and County road crews spent days cutting grass along the roads, leveling out the parking areas, and finally spreading gravel on them and on the roads. Even the gravel, both coarse and fine shale, was donated. A local construction company stockpiled the shale for the camp. Army Reserve units spent several weekends at Kleenburn trimming trees and leveling banks.

Scout leaders built the twelve tables, but everything down to the last bolt, as well as the cement to hold them, was donated, as were garbage barrels and fireplace grates. A local well driller even drilled a well at no charge.

Cub and Boy Scouts worked weekends clearing brush, painting, and trying out the fishing holes. Scout leaders found the boys could work here on a variety of merit badges pertaining to wildlife, plants and conservation. When Camporees were scheduled the camp was a perfect place for contests—from fishing to racing.

Cash gifts were used to rent equipment and to purchase paint and other items not donated. The sign hanging over Kleenburn Camp was built by a shop class at the high school with material paid for by a long time Scout leader. The sign was erected by the State Highway Department.

Originally, the camp was open for all groups in the community with the Boy Scout committee in charge of the calendar, and having priority for Scouting events. However, due to a wave of vandalism, it was necessary to lock the gate, leaving a phone number to call for group reservations. In spite of this inconvenience many groups have used the camp for summer picnics, class reunions, and family get togethers.

What about the future of Kleenburn Camp? By careful planning the reclamation of the camp site will be spread over a period of years, so that other generations of Boy Scouts can say, ''I had a part in Kleenburn Camp, and we have restored a damaged area to its natural beauty.''

Photo Courtesy of Dave Graunke

I would like to challenge you with two questions. The first was written by Thomas Jefferson in 1820:

"I know no safe depository of the ultimate powers of the society but the people themselves; and if we think them not enlightened enough to exercise their control with a wholesome discretion, the remedy is not to take it from them, but to inform their discretion."

The second was stated by Stephanie Mills of Zero Population Growth in 1970, 150 years later:

"The only kind of power people can have without informing themselves is destructive power. It is important to question everything not to accept anything at face value."1

I have long been interested in the problem of communicating messages between our increasingly proliferated technology, and the great lay public who will be affected by that technology. As a past case I cite the problem of educating the public to the nature and ramifications of nuclear energy, whether as a weapon or an industry, following World War II. As a present case, I'd cite the cultural ripples beginning to be felt from the so-called biological revolution: artificial insemination, ectogenesis, cloning, genetic tampering, and all the other innovative techniques in reproductive biology.

It seems to me that public knowledge of the terminology and as many basic concepts of contemporary science as possible, cannot help but dilute the effects of what Alvin Toffler has termed "Future Shock." I feel it imperative that as much knowledge about technology and insight into science be disseminated on as broad a base as is possible. I think this should be a central concern of today. Both individually and collectively, as communities, we face a multitude of possible futures. To a degree always difficult to determine, we exercise some amount of choice over our own destinies. We do have alternatives from which to decide, but an accelerating river of information about our alternatives is passing us by. Like the caucus race in *Alice in Wonderland*, we must run ever faster just to stay even with the current.

I am a professional writer. Most of what I write is labeled "science fiction;" and so, I suppose, I am therefore a *de facto* science fiction writer. Science fiction is both an extremely popular informational medium these days, and is also characterized as a literature of alternatives.

In discussing possible futures for Wyoming communities, particularly as they will be affected by alternative sources of power, I want to discuss science fiction as a legitimate companion to futurology, as well as a popular and publically accessible form of communication.

In an essay called "Man's Adaptation to Change," Dr. Alan E. Nourse says: "Science fiction today is still essentially a popular escape literature, unsophisticated and amusement-oriented. What, then, makes it so useful as a device to ease and abet man's adaptation to change? First, as opposed to mystery novels, western novels, popular love novels, sports stories, or other forms of popular fiction, science fiction is primarily a literature of ideas. Quite aside from its entertainment value, science fiction stimulates the speculative imagination. The reader of a science fiction story is invited to suspend his disbelief and embark upon and adventure dealing with events and propositions that have not yet happened but which might very conceivably occur at some time in the future, be it tomorrow or a thousand years hence. Typically a science fiction story begins with a premise which may be untrue but is at least plausible."2

The Wages of Synergy is Life

Edward Bryant
Denver

Hence the bedrock of science or speculative fiction is extrapolation. Extrapolation is simply the gathering together of known factors, if possible adding one or more random variables or "wild cards," then projecting the emergent pattern into the future. The process is usually a good deal more complicated than the definition.

The underlying assumption of the extrapolative process is that things *are* going to change. Dr.

Nourse asks: "How can a popular literature which is often regarded as 'crazy' or 'fantastic' by those least acquainted with it actually equip its readers to adapt to social, cultural, or technological change? First and foremost, science fiction prepares the minds of its readers with certain concepts or attitudes toward change that are not always widely shared by others. For example, the science fiction reader is powerfully acclimatized to the underlying idea that change is going to come about, come what may. There is no nonsense in his head about resisting, thwarting, or evading change. The science fiction stories that he reads dwell upon future societies that *have* changed from the present. In these stories change is regarded as inevitable; indeed, science fiction frequently predicates that rapid, radical, or abrupt change as probable in the pattern of the future."[3]

Social resistance to change is one of the great givens in this society founded, ironically enough, by an armed and active revolution. People rarely like to hear about the things which may change the status quo, expecially for the worse. That's one reason why fiction affords a more subtle route to communicating information to the public about their possible futures.

Frank Herbert, active in ecological work and author of the ecological novel *Dune,* writes about this issue of change, and then transmutes it to the issue of synergy:

"On this relatively small planet well out into the edge of a minor spiral galaxy, we have been simultaneously breeding ourselves an abundance of humans while creating an abundance of material things for a small proportion of that burgeoning life. Against a backdrop of false absolutes, we reduce the variables that we permit in our societies, in our individuals, and in our possessions. By our acts, we demonstrate that we want mass production of a standard human who employs standardized consumer goods. We execute this mass production sameness in a largely unexamined, unconscious manner.

"But nature constantly evolves, trying out its new arrangements, its new kinds of life, its differences, its interesting times, its crises. Against such movement, we attempt our balancing acts, our small sallies at equilibrium. In the dynamic interrelationships of the universe around us, we look for models upon which to pattern our lives. But that universe greets us with complexities everywhere we turn. To talk about just one element, carbon, for example, we are forced to deal with combinations whose complexities we have not yet exhausted.

"You've read about such things in science fiction; you see the conditions around you which touch your own life. Still, you seek *the* answer."[4]

There is, of course, no such thing as *the* answer. In our future Wyoming, there is probably no single power source which will fuel our engines or heat our homes for tomorrow; no solar nor wind, geothermal nor nuclear fusion. And not, God forbid, coal fueled electrical plants or nuclear fission. Such answers as will come about, such patterns as emerge from our experiments in extrapolation, will be complex. They will be systems, approaches, combinations; and such answers will take a synergistic position. Synergy: two or more factors in a system working cooperatively together...and often with the connotation that the whole is indeed greater than the sum of the parts.

Thus the title of this article: "The Wages of Synergy is Life," a somewhat paraphrase of *Romans, VI, 3.* Our collective tomorrow is multiplex by any reasonable expectation; and if Laramie is primarily to be powered by wind, and Thermopolis by wet steam field geothermal energy, and Wheatland by coal-fired electrical power, and all of them supplemented by an energy grid from a pilot fusion plant near Casper, then so be it. We will survive cooperatively or we probably shall not survive at all.

Synergistics, change, extrapolation; thus far, three key words.

To quote Alan Nourse again: "Science fiction prepares its readers for successful adaptation to change first by accepting the fact of change, whether desirable or not, as inevitable; second, by seeking to adjust to the change wherever possible; and third by modifying the change when possible or necessary in order to reduce its negative impact on our lives.

"The non adaptive individual is frightened by the unfamiliar and seeks unsuccessfully to resist it. The science fiction reader is dealing constantly with the unfamiliar and is equally, and success-fully, seeking familiar patterns or trends in it.

"Thus we can say that science fiction engenders a positive adaptive attitude in the minds of its readers. What is more, it furthers adaptation toward change by developing in its readers the elasticity of mind—the sheer imaginative grasp—to enable them to grapple with change construc-tively. The typical science fiction reader is capable of conceiving many possible futures, each different from the other, and is comfortable dealing with change one step at a time in approaching these possible futures."[5]

I don't claim that science fiction readers, as a group necessarily are attuned to the sense of change, the flexible adaptiveness that will assure immunity from future shock. Science fiction readers can be as stodgy and imaginatively immovable as the most flagrant coal company... and occasionally environmental group...public relations person. But that doesn't detract from the potential of science fiction as a communicative medium. It has a deep inherent capacity for carrying information, sometimes propagandistic, nearly always didactic.

"There is a tradition in modern physics known as the "*gedankenexperiment*," a term coined by the German physicist Heisenberg. The term means literally "thought experiment" and describes a mental experiment in which the physicist imagines a precise set of experimental conditions or sets up a well-defined series of assumptions and tries to infer logically the results of the experiment.

"Science fiction has often shown a remarkable ability to forsee technological developments in its' *gedankenexperimenten* even though it has been somewhat less successful in anticipating social and political changes."6 More, its function as a framework for the imaginary experiment has been formalized in "such government supported 'think tanks' as the Institute for Defense Analysis and Dr. Herman Kahn's Hudson Institute. This latter institute has for years been engaged in writing scenarios projecting a series of alternative futures, depending on possible developments in the social and political forces now at work."

The most common *gedankenexperimenten* in science fiction have been simple utopias or dystopias, anti utopias. Utopias, trying to be templates showing you just how good things could be if only a few factors were altered, tend to be less effective and less popular than their negative counterparts. Let me cite B.F. Skinner's *Walden Two* as against, say, *1984* by George Orwell. I suspect the reason may be that archetypical utopias tend to reflect the idealized theories of a small group or even of a single man or woman; but memorable dystopias mirror shared terrors, our collective paranoias of authoritarian government, monitored lives, or ecological breakdown.

It can be debated how much measurable effect such books have. No metric scale for empirical effects of literature has yet been devised. Yet I'd argue in the corner of those believing that very often *the word* comes first, and then is reflected in the actions of society, rather than the other way around.

As practically every eighth grader knows, or at least is told—the single most catalytic novel of time, in terms of precipitating social action, was *Uncle Tom's Cabin*. There is no *Uncle Tom's Cabin* in science fiction yet. But there are science fiction scenarios closely linking today and our tomorrows. Take, for example, the overcrowded rat population experiment. Translated into real terms, it approaches closer than Calcutta or Bombay. It's right next door in Rock Springs and Green River. Consider the annual growth rate since 1970 of 19 per cent, the pressures on schools and law enforcement agencies and city services, the endless trailer camps, the constantly eroding quality of life. Consider any of the so-called impact areas, such as Gillette. Did you know there is an increasingly popular psychological term for the effects of overcrowding called the "Gillette Syndrome?" These things are translated fictionally into such novels as Robert Silverberg's *The World Inside*, or Harry Harrison's *Make Room, Make Room*, from which the inept film *Soylent Green* was derived.

Silverberg, incidentally, created a scenario for the reclamation of our ecologically devastated world in a short story called "The Wind and the Rain." The story takes place millennia in the future when an intelligent race from another solar system comes to ours to reclaim the long dead Earth. One of the characters, in toting up the reasons for Earth's perishing, lists a contributing cause as the uncontrolled release of methane into the atmosphere. Silverberg notes that the growth of human population produced a consequent increase in the supply of methane. As one of his characters describes it, "The surplus methane escaped into the lower stratosphere from ten to thirty miles above the surface of the planet, where a layer of ozone molecules once existed. Ozone, formed of three oxygen atoms, absorbs the harmful ultraviolet radiation that the sun emits. By reacting with free oxygen atoms in the stratosphere, the intrusive methane reduced the quantity available for ozone formation. Moreover, methane reactions in the stratosphere yielded water vapor that further depleted the ozone. This methane-induced exhaustion of the ozone content of the stratosphere permitted the unchecked ultraviolet bombardment of the Earth, with a consequent rise in the incidence of skin cancer."7

A partial bibliography of avouedly fictional scenarios would include *Nerves*, Lester Del Rey's novel of a massive accident in a nuclear power plant; Frank Herbert's famous *Dune*, the epic novel of a desert world; John Brunner's prophetic and finely detailed novels *Stand on Zanzibar* and *The Sheep Look Up*. There are also such theme anthologies as *Voyages: Scenarios for a Ship called Earth*, published by Ballantine Books and ZPG; *The Wounded Planet*, originally published as *Saving Worlds*; and a book called *Eco-Fiction*.

The purpose of these books, beyond entertainment, is succinctly stated in John Stadler's introduction to *Eco-Fiction*: I hope this anthology will encourage some serious thinking. I have been struck by some repeated themes. The first is that men do not listen to warnings. The second is that if men hear the warnings they do not heed them; we do nothing. The third is that we should not let ourselves be paralyzed into idleness by the vastness and complexity of our ecological problems. Ecological catastrophes seem to begin in small, simple, controllable actions. The last theme is that solutions, like the problems themselves, may have their beginnings in the small and simple acts of individual men (and women)."[7]

Concomitant with what Mr. Stadler has to say, I think, is the implicit idea that we are all, each one of us, responsible for his or her acts. And thus must be aware of the ramification of our actions—or our inactions.

Basically, I agree with Mr. Stadler's sober thoughts, though I am slightly more optimistic about the possibility of generating or catalyzing action. Or, at the very least, of stirring thought, debate, and possibly, resultant action. But I'll point out that scenarios and stories, futurologists and science fiction writers cannot claim the answers. At best, we hope we can provide some alternatives. And then *all* of us, informed and judicious, will choose the right answers. Hopefully.

As a parting observation, I'd like to forecast that Wyoming is going to find itself increasingly center-stage in contemporary writing, both science-fictional and otherwise. I don't think it really hyperbolic to suggest that Wyoming is a microcosm for the immense and rapid changes radically transforming the Rocky Mountain region, and by extension the rest of the nation, through the end of this century. We're all of us riding the cutting edge of the future. And if science fiction, as one agent of adaptation, can help us flex with change without breaking, then good luck to us all. We'll need it.[8]

Notes

1. Stephanie Mills, *Voyages; Scenarios for a Ship Called Earth,* New York: Ballantine Books, 1971, p. xvii.

2. Alan E. Nourse, "SF and Man's Adaptation to Change," from *Science Fiction, Today and Tomorrow*, edited by Reginald Bretnor, New York: Harper & Row, 1974, p. 120.

3. Ibid.

4. Frank Herbert, "SF and a World in Crisis," from *Science Fiction, Today and Tomorrow,* edited by Reginald Bretnor, New York: Harper & Row, 1974, p. 77.

5. Nourse, *op. cit.,* p. 125.

6. Thomas Scortia, "Science Fiction as the Imaginary Experiment," from *Science Fiction, Today and Tomorrow,* edited by Reginald Bretnor, New York; Harper & Row, 1974, p. 137.

7. Robert Silverberg, "The Wind and the Rain," in *The Wounded Planet,* edited by Roger Elwood and Virginia Kidd, New York: Doubleday, 1973, pp. 226, 227.

8. This article is excerpted and condensed from a presentation to "A Play on Power," an alternative energy futures conference, Rawlins, Wyoming, 24 May 1975.

Beyond the Sand River Range

Edward Bryant

Calvin Knifehunter rode down out of the Sand River Range with his back to the north wind and his face to the cold stars. Wind rushed powerfully through the stands of blue spruce as the horse picked a trail down the slope. The wind shouted and Cal listened to it, ignoring the cold.

A rock dislodged under the horse's hoof and the animal's hindquarters slipped downhill as it struggled to keep equilibrium. The horse found its balance.

"Easy, girl." Below, the rattle of sliding stones diminished in the darkness. The rider nudged the mare's ribs with his heel. "Come on."

The moon began to rise as the land became level. The bleakness of the open range was softened by moonlight. The timber thinned and disappeared, but the wind remained strong as Cal rode through the low sagebrush.

There was a fence of barbed wire and a tightly stretched gate, then the last pasture before home. The mare knew she was going home and broke into a gallop. Cal rode bareback and he felt the rhythm of the horse's muscles.

Across a dry creek bed and then the dark outbuildings. Cal swung down off the mare. The horse whickered, breathing heavily, and there was foam in her jaws.

"You've had a good vacation, right, girl? You aren't used to this." Cal led the mare into the small barn. He gave her a cursory rubdown and part of a pail of oats. Then he walked to the house.

The collie, Brownie, tail wagging, waited for him on the porch. Cal knelt and rubbed between the dog's ears. The man looked up at the empty rocking chair in back of Brownie. He remembered his father endlessly rocking in that chair, growing older until he died of old age at forty-six. The rocker remained, but the empty bottles had long since been thrown away.

The door opened into light and warmth. Preceded by Brownie, Cal walked into the three-room house. His mother sat reading at the table beneath the unshaded hundred-watt bulb.

Leah Marshall Knifehunter was a tired woman. She had never been pretty, but many who knew her as a girl had attributed to her what they called "spunk." She had been the daughter of a town banker in Fremont and was theoretically fated to marry high up in the aristocracy of the rural West. But chance and unexplainable impulse had intervened and Leah married Thomas Eagle Feather Knifehunter, full-blooded Shoshoni. That she "married Indian" was unforgivable. She was written out of her father's will. She was ostracized by her white friends. She was only grudgingly accepted by the Indians of the reservation. Leah had married for love.

"Was it like you remember?"

Cal sat down opposite his mother. "Yes. Four years doesn't change much up there." He was suddenly aware of the numbness in his fingers. He rubbed his hands together to warm them. "Babe's fat and lazy now. Needs to be ridden. I'll work it off her."

"You hungry?"

Cal considered. "No."

"Some venison steaks. Deer your Uncle Paul shot last winter."

"No thanks. Just not hungry. I'm going into Fremont for a while."

"Why?" There was a strange note in Leah's voice.

"Thought I'd look up some old friends."

"Be careful."

Cal laughed. "Mom, I'm not going to get in trouble. I'm a college graduate now, remember?"

His mother, grimly, "Aren't many of your old friends left."

"I know." The laughter left his voice. "But some of them aren't dead or in jail."

"Be home early?"

"Probably." His words were light again. "Mom, I'm not your baby any more."

"I know." She hesitated. "But be careful anyway."

"I will," he said, standing and taking the car keys from the table. "Keep Brownie inside until I'm gone." The last thing he saw as he closed the door was the row of old books on the shelf across the room. Worn spines and faded gilt titles: Rousseau and Bunyan, *The Book of Martyrs* and Thoreau.

The '55 Chevy bounced noisily along the two miles of ruts that joined the state highway. Cal thought of his mother making her weekly shopping trips to Fremont in this car.

Twenty miles he drove along Sand River Canyon. There was very little traffic, so he pushed the protesting engine until the car vibrated along at seventy. Then the highway angled around the flank of a mountain and Cal saw the lights of Fremont ahead. Fremont, county seat of Shoshoni County. Commercial center for the ranching community, for the reservation, for the uranium

Photo Courtesy of Peggy McDonald

45

and oil people. Five thousand nice white Anglo souls, Cal thought, and wished he could work the medicine which would bring the Sand River Range sliding down on Fremont.

He was vaguely surprised at his gut reaction. Hatred, Cal thought. Maybe school didn't civilize me as much as it was intended.

The lights of Fremont grew brighter and more distinct. The road ran down a slight grade, then across the seldom-used railroad tracks and into Main Street. Downtown Fremont was five blocks of light and noise; stores, filling stations and bars. At ten o'clock on this October night, the stores were closed. But it was the third Saturday in the month. The men from the oil fields had their pay. So did the hands off the local ranches. And the Indians had their government checks.

Cal parked a block off Main and locked the car. He walked through the downtown, seeing many faces, but none familiar. Cal was suddenly thirsty and decided to get a beer.

"Hey, you! Injun! You with the funny hair!" The shout was from behind him. Cal took his hand away from the door to the Antelope Lounge and slowly turned. His fingers curled into fists. Then he involuntarily stared and pulled a doubletake. "Davy! I'll be damned."

"Hey man, you look good." Davy White Hawk walked forward grinning and holding out his hand.

"Long time," Cal said.

"Yeah, you home from school for good?"

"A while, maybe. Probably a year. I'm in VISTA now—be working out on the reservation. Then I figure the government'll send me to law school."

"Hey, you'll be the biggest success the tribe ever had."

"Maybe."

"You will; no sweat. How about a beer to celebrate?"

"That's what I was after when you yelled."

"At the Antelope? Hell, let's go down to the Wagon Box. They got the wildest go-go dancer you ever saw."

"I don't know," said Cal. He hesitated. "I remember before I left, the Wagon Box was kind of a hassle."

"Yeah." Davy was expressionless. "Things are different now. A little. They'll let anybody in, if they have the money."

The bar was crowded and noisy. The hostess, fifty and wrinkled in red velvet, showed them to a small table close to the juke box.

"I don't think I missed much!" Cal shouted,

competing with eighty decibels of Buck Owens.

"Must be the girl's taking a break," said Davy. The barmaid set a pitcher and two glasses down hard on the table, slopping beer on Coors napkins.

"Davy, what are you doing these days?"

"Not much." He poured carefully, not allowing a head to foam on the beer. "This and that. You know."

"Yeah, I know."

Someone lurched against the table and a wave of alcoholic breath made Cal think of a rotting carcass under the sun. By his stained work clothes a wildcatter down from the drilling rigs in the hills, the man surveyed Cal and Davy with bleary eyes. "Hey, boys," he said, slurring the 's.' "What time you dance?"

Davy half rose, pulling back his right fist. Cal stood and grabbed his arm. "No," Cal said. "Come on."

Outside, Cal said, "Maybe things haven't changed."

"Maybe not." Davy's jaw was set tense; the skin stretched tight over high cheekbones. "We should have killed that son-of-a-bitch."

And it all flowed back through Cal's memory, as if borne by the wind which lashed around the mercury street lamps.

Four years before. The rain had fallen in sporadic showers of large, chill drops, settling finally to a steady drizzle. The gray thunderheads had rolled, been torn apart by the wind and reunited high over the Sand Rivers. And at two in the morning, Davy's little sister Mickey had stumbled through the puddles to the Knifehunter house.

Davy needed help, she had said. They were looking for Richard, their older brother. He had gone to Fremont in the afternoon for groceries. He hadn't come back. Awakened at midnight, a sleepy grocer claimed indignantly on the phone that he hadn't seen Richard White Hawk at all. So Davy started the search.

It was Cal, Davy, and Lattimer, the Indian Agent, who found him finally. As they rounded a rainslick curve by the canyon, the brights picked up a reflected gleam that could have been the eyes of an animal. They braked and looked closer and saw the skid marks black under the sheet of rain. They parked Lattimer's big Oldsmobile on the shoulder of the state highway and let the lights play on the shining object. Ungracefully the three slid down the slick grass of the embankment.

"Over here!"

The object was a chrome hubcap from a Ford pickup. The three probed beyond and turned on their flashlights. They found the truck itself about forty yards further. It lay upside down, masked from the road by clumps of tall willows.

Sick at what he knew he would find, Cal pushed ahead of Davy and shone his light in the cab. Richard was still there. Sprawled half out the window of the cab, he had been pinned by the crushed roof. He lay face down. The coroner said at the inquest that Richard White Hawk had drowned in an inch of muddy water. The ruling had been accidental death as a result of driving while intoxicated (there was a half-empty fifth of cheap whisky under the seat).

But before that, on the stormy mountainside, Davy had found a deeper reason for his brother's death. He had knelt and lifted his brother's head out of the puddled rain and cradled it silently for a few minutes. Then he had looked up at Lattimer, his face as rigid as the Sand River granite.

"You did this," he said to the Indian Agent. And that was all.

Four years later, Cal remembered the white man's eyes, pitying and paternal, as they looked silently away.

You did this, Cal's mind had echoed. Three words too simple, but sufficient. And he knew then he would do anything, even go to the white man's college, to keep it from happening again.

"Hello, Cal."

Cal looked back and saw the same eyes, four years older, surrounded by more wrinkles but the same blue eyes. "Hello," he said.

Donald Lattimer was a career man in the Bureau of Indian Affairs. He was a kind man, and a conscientious man, and he did for "his people" what he thought was right. But he was white and from a prosperous timber family in Wisconsin and there were many things about this job which he could never know.

The Indian Agent walked up to them, smiling. "Hello, Davy."

"Excuse me, I got to see somebody. See you, Cal." He turned and hurried down the sidewalk.

"We sure are proud of you, son," Lattimer said, pumping Cal's hand enthusiastically. "And coming back to help your people—, well, all we can say is, that's great."

"Yeah," come off it, thought Cal.

The white man looked wary. "You still dislike me, don't you Cal."

"Yes."

"Why?"

Cal didn't answer.

Lattimer said, "Son, you're too much a romantic. You're really caught up emotionally in your people's whole tradition and history. Don't fight the war that ended long ago."

"I am?"

"It's over. We're not the same people who drove you out of your forests and plains and broke the treaties."

Cal was suddenly, unaccountably angry. "No? How many names should I call out? Wounded Knee, 1890. Three hundred Sioux civililans, men, women and children, massacred by U.S. troopers. Times have changed? Check your newspapers, man."

Lattimer's expression was patient. "When you were on that scholarship in California, did you take an anthropology course?"

"Yes."

"And do you remember learning anything about two cultures on a collision course?"

Cal realized he might have underestimated the man. He said, as though quoting the textbook, "In a conflict of two societies, the technologically superior culture usually emerges dominant."

"Not *usually*, Cal. *Always*. History bears that out."

"No!"

Lattimer looked down at the dirty, cracked pavement. "Part of the losing culture may survive; often it may subvert a part of victor. But its culture, as an entire pattern, is smashed." He raised his head and looked Cal in the eye. "That happens and both sides have to accept it. They have to work with it."

Cal's words were very low and clear. "Man, you're arrogant. So godamned arrogant. And someday it's going to bring you down."

"I'm sorry. I'm just trying to be honest."

Something was wrong. Cal looked around and realized he and Lattimer were alone on the street. There was a metallic rattle as the wind drove an empty aluminum beer can down the sidewalk. It rolled against Cal's boot and stopped.

Down the block the door of the Antelope Lounge opened and Davy White Hawk ran down the street toward them.

"Where is everybody?" Cal yelled.

"Inside. Watching TV in the bars. Man, you're missing it. Biggest show of the century." Davy was gasping, out of breath.

"What's this?" said Lattimer.

"News show, every channel. Goddamn aliens."

"Aliens?" Lattimer looked puzzled.

"Space people, somebody. Flying saucer or something. Big round thing, glows white, big as a goddam mountain. Landed outside New York."

For once Lattimer's fatherly composure was disturbed. "This is true?"

Davy stared. "So help me, it's true. Big goddamn round thing. TV says it's from another star or something. Scientists figure they're maybe thousands of years ahead of us."

The wind rose and whistled around the cornices of the Shoshoni County Courthouse on the next block.

"A thousand years ahead," said Cal

Lattimer was not an unintelligent man. He understood when Cal looked up at the cold stars above the Sand River Range and began to laugh.

Reprinted from the anthology
INFINITY THREE, Robert Hoskins.
Lancer Books, Inc.

Illustration by Joan Malone

Vernon James Puckett Goes to the Moon

Shirley B. Nix
Casper

Vernon James Puckett went to the Moon on Saturday morning. It was a good day for a trip to the Moon because there is no school on Saturday. He went to the Moon in a spacebox he built in his back yard. His grandfather gave him the box. It was bigger than Vernon James and he could sit inside of it. His mother gave him a peanut butter sandwich in a paper bag.

His mother said, ''Have a good time on the Moon. Remember where your home is and don't be late for supper!''

I know my home is on Badger Street,'' said Vernon James. ''I won't be late for supper. Good-bye!''

Vernon James looked at the grass and trees in his back yard. He climbed into his spacebox and flew for a very long time. He ate his peanut butter sandwich. Then, he fell asleep in his spacebox.

When Vernon James opened his eyes, he knew he was not in his back yard on Badger Street. There was no grass and there were no trees. He knew he was not on the Moon because there were no craters. Vernon James knew very well where he was NOT, but he did not know where he WAS. He thought he was lost.

The deep blue sky was all around him. Winking, blinking lights flew this way and that way. Vernon James was puzzled. He did not know which way to fly to Badger Street and he though he would be late for supper.

Just then, KERPLUNK! A box landed right beside him. Vernon James was so surprised, he jumped and almost upset his spacebox. The new box was the biggest one Vernon James had ever seen—in it a friendly, brown face with sparkling, brown eyes. He wore a bright green space suite and a bright green cap. There was a gold badge on his cap.

He smiled and said, "Welcome to space! I am the Traffic Director of the Universe. It is against the rules to park your spacebox in the sky on Saturday. There are too many spaceboxes buzzing around the Universe on Saturday."

Vernon James nodded his head. He said, "Yes, Sir. I am Vernon James Puckett, Sir. I was going to the Moon today but, I fell asleep. Now, I think I am lost and I will be late for supper. Can you direct me to my home on Badger Street, please?"

The Traffic Director said, "Yes, I can. Let me see your flight plan."

Vernon James was puzzled. "I don't have a flight plan," he said. "What is a flight plan?"

The Traffic Director frowned. "My goodnes," he said, "A flight plan shows you where you are going, Vernon James Puckett. My goodness, if you can't find where you are going, you can't fly to any of your homes!"

"But, Sir," said Vernon James, "I only have ONE home. My home is on Badger Street."

"No, no," said the Traffic Director. He sounded very cross. "EVERYONE has lots of homes."

Vernon James was just a little bit afraid of the Traffic Director. He did not want him to be angry, but he KNEW he had only one home and he said so.

The Traffic Director began to grumble. "That's the trouble with the Universe on Saturday. There are too many spaceboxes flying around with no flight plans and EVERY, SINGLE pilot thinks he has ONE, SINGLE home. "Follow me," he snapped. "You have to make a flight plan and you can do it in my office on the Moon."

Without another word, he sat down in his spacebox and flew away!

Vernon James followed the Traffic Director as fast as he could. He did not really want to go to the space office, even if it WAS on the Moon. He really wanted to go home for supper, but after all, he was lost. Maybe, thought Vernon James, if I do EXACTLY what he tells me, I can find Badger Street.

They flew very fast. Z-I-I-I-P! Z-I-I-I-P! The Traffic Director seemed to know where he was going. KERPLUNK! KERPLUNK! Vernon James knew they were on the Moon when they landed, because there were craters everywhere. He wanted to look around and see more of the Moon, but, the Traffic Director was still very cross.

"Hurry up, Vernon James Puckett," he grumbled. "I can't spend all my time helping you. Saturday is a very busy day for me."

They climbed down a gold ladder into a very large crater. The crater looked like an office, but, everything was gold and there was no roof at all! There was a gold chair and a gold desk. There was a large map on one of the gold walls. The Traffic Director told Vernon James to sit in the gold chair and gave him a pencil and paper.

"Now, " said the Traffic Director, "I will show you how to make a flight plan. Then, you will know you have LOTS of homes. I will ask questions and you must write the answers on the paper. The answers are your flight plan."

Vernon James nodded his head. He did NOT think he had lots of homes and he DID think he was going to be late for supper. But, he had to find his way back to Badger Street.

"What is a home?" asked the Traffic Director.

That's a silly question, thought Vernon James. He said, "Home is where I live," and he wrote it on the paper.

The Traffic Director pointed to the large map. "This is a map of the Universe," he said. "Do you live in the Universe?"

Vernon James knew he lived in the Universe, so he nodded his head again.

The Traffic Director said, "Then, the Universe is home number ONE. Write it on your paper." and, Vernon James did.

There were several globes in a far corner of the gold office. Each globe was as big as THREE BEACH BALLS! The Traffic Director pointed to the globes and said, "These globes look like the planets in the Universe. The planet you live on is your home planet. Do you know the name of your home planet?"

Vernon James began to smile. Flight plans were puzzles and he liked puzzles. He thought he knew now why he had lots of homes. The Earth was the planet he lived on and it was home number TWO. He wrote it on his flight plan.

Then, the Traffic Director chose one of the very

large globes and set it on the gold floor. Vernon James knew it was the Planet Earth. It looked like the globe at school, only it was much larger. The Traffic Director told him that the Planet Earth had several continents. The next name on the puzzle was a continent!

Vernon James turned the very large globe round and round. He had to think for a long time. At last, he remembered. He lived on the Continent of North America and he found it on the globe. That was home number THREE!

The Traffic Director was not a bit cross, now. His brown eyes sparkled as he looked at the flight plan. He said, "You are doing very well, Vernon James Puckett! Now, you know you live in the Universe, on the Planet Earth, on the Continent of North America. That is ONE, TWO, THREE homes. You will need SEVEN homes for your flight plan. Find them if you can!" And, he waved at Vernon James and climbed up the gold ladder.

Vernon James thought and thought. He had THREE homes and he had to have SEVEN homes. He needed FOUR more homes. He looked at the Continent of North American on the globe. "HA!" he shouted. "NOW I KNOW! There are countries in continents. Home number FOUR is my country and that is the United States of America!" That was easy, he thought, and he wrote it one his flight plan.

Vernon James found the United States of America, on the Continent of North America, on the Planet Earth, in the Universe. He was SURE he could finish his flight plan. He knew his country was divided into states. He found the State of New York and the State of California and the State of Texas. Then, he found the State of WYOMING! THAT WAS IT! He lived in the State of Wyoming and it was home number FIVE. Maybe, thought Vernon James, just maybe, I won't be late for supper after all.

Cities and towns are in states and he knew he lived in the City of Casper. He found it almost in the middle of the State of Wyoming. It was home number SIX.

He had to find ONE more home and it was Badger Street. The street names were very, very small. Vernon James looked and looked. THERE IT WAS! Vernon James found Badger Street, in the City of Casper, in the State of Wyoming, in the United States of America, on the Continent of North America on the Planet Earth, in the Universe. Badger Street was home number SEVEN, HURRAY!

Vernon James ran to the gold ladder and climbed out of the gold office. The Traffic Director was waiting for him.

"Here it is!" shouted Vernon James. "Here is my flight plan and I have ALL SEVEN HOMES on it. I have lots of homes and I want to go to home number SEVEN!"

The Traffic Director laughed and said, "Good for you, Vernon James Puckett!" He pointed his finger. "Fly that way to the Planet Earth. You can't miss it because it looks EXACTLY like the globe in my gold office.
Just follow your flight plan and you will get to home number SEVEN in time for your supper."

Vernon James said, "Thank you very much, Mister Traffic Director. I know EXACTLY how to find home number SEVEN. May I come back to the Moon next Saturday?"

"Yes, indeed," said the Traffic Director. "Just remember, you MUST have a flight plan."

Vernon James climbed into his spacebox, waved to the Traffic Director and flew away to the Planet Earth. Z-I-I-I-P!

He had no trouble finding the Planet Earth and when he found it, he flew around and around it until he saw the Continent of North America. He flew over North America and saw the United States of America. He flew slower until he found the State of Wyoming. Then, he flew very slowly, indeed, until he saw the City of Casper. Back and forth, he flew, over the City of Casper and, at last, Vernon James found home number SEVEN. There was his very own house on Badger Street.

KERPLUNK! He landed in the back yard and ran into the house. "Guess what? he said. "I am back from the Moon. Am I late for supper?"

His mother said, "You are ALMOST late for supper. Did you forget who you are and where you live?"

Vernon James said, "I am Vernon James Pucket. I live on Badger Street in the City of Casper, in the State of Wyoming, in the United States of America, on the Continent of North America, on the Planet Earth, in the Universe. I have SEVEN homes and I know how to make a flight plan, too!"

His mother said, "Wash your hands, Vernon James Puckett. It is time for supper."

Fremont Peak and Mount Sacajawea in the Wind River Range. Milky Lake in the foreground.

Solitude

Nancy Curtis
Glendo

Does solitude

Amidst the quiet splendor

Of mountain sundown

Bare reflected deities

Who unearth my soul?

A tanka is a form of Japanese poetry which is about nature, usually one sentence, and loosely based on 5-7-5-7-5 syllables.

Frosted Corn

Early frost that sears the growing corn
Transforms the pliant leaves to brittle files.
    Then comes the pitiless wind to rustle them
    And make them rattle like the loose-hung
    bones
    Of family skeletons in webby closets.

On all the earth there is no sadder sound
Though I should saddle up and chase the wind
around.
    But when the winds have lulled to wistful
    zephers
    The corn-blades sigh and whisper
    "Rest now. Rest."

Myra Connell
Lander

Reprinted from Wyoming Electric News

Wyoming Women

INTRODUCTION

Equal rights for women didn't come to Wyoming with any amendment or legislation. They didn't even come with votes for women, though we were the first state who granted that. Women were equal to their men from the moment the first pioneers settled here. They worked just as hard and side by side with their husbands in the fields and on the range. They shared equally in the responsibilities, the dangers, hardships, and the triumphs as Wyoming changed from a territory to a state and from a wilderness to a rich ranch land.

From Nellie Tayloe Ross, the first woman governor in any state to Cattle Kate, the first woman, so far as we can determine to be hanged for cattle stealing, Wyoming women have been liberated and "equal."

To prove it, here are the stories of two women from the Salt Creek area.

R.C.

Women's Liberation came late to Salt Creek.

Velva Mattix
Midwest

Women's Lib came too late to Salt Creek, for women in this area of the Equality State have long been doing anything *HE* can do.

Take Brida Gafford for one, as she was Rodeo's first Lady Bronc Rider, winning the World's Championship three times.

At seventy-nine years of age, she still lives close to Lusk, Wy. on a homestead twenty-six miles northeast of the Salt Creek Oil Field. Until recently she ran, single-handedly, her sprawling 1,280 acre ranch.

Still lean and limber, Brida sports the western costume she wore thirty-eight years ago in Madison Square Garden when she won the World's Championship.

Born in LaCross, Wisconsin, in 1896, Brida went to live with her grandparents when she was nine. "I felt I had too much bossing around and a year later, I ran away from home. Of course, my grandparents brought me right back, but every time I'd get mad at my grandmother I would threaten to run away and join the circus as a lady rider. I always loved horses and started riding at the age of two."

Brida thought that she and horses belonged together, but when she ran away from home for good, at age 13, she took a train. Her grandfather, in a vain attempt to keep her in school long enough to get her past the fourth grade, had given

55

her $50 for school clothes and books as an incentive, but Brida absconded with the funds and bought a ticket for Miles City, Montana—to what she figured would be a gay, new life in the romantic Wild West.

The romance paled when she arrived at the station in Miles City, alone, broke, hungry, and with no one to meet her. With no place to go and nothing to do, she stood at the station window making pictures on the window panes, and crying. An elderly gentlemen, named Turner, noticed her and inquired whose little girl she was. Brida answered, "I'm nobody's little girl." Turner took her to his wife and the couple gave her a home for a time.

Then, one Billy Richardson, took note of Brida's riding ability and proclaimed that she was just a "natural" on a horse and he got her started at racing in flat races. Later he tried her on a bronc and found she could stick like glue.

In 1910, Brida entered her first rodeo bronc riding contest and, "got bumped off on my head," she said ruefully, "but I won second in the flat races."

From that time on, she rode in races and did exhibition bronc riding at ten to twenty-five dollars a ride.

At age seventeen, she married Henry Shimek and they moved to a farm in Nebraska, which they ran until he died in the flu epidemic following World War I. Brida tried to hold onto the farm but lost out and came to Lusk, Wyoming. She leased 160 acres of land and put in thirty acres of potatoes. Seed potatoes cost her eight dollars per hundred pounds. When the crops were grown, the prices had dropped until she could not give away the "spuds." She left 1,500 bushels in the fields.

Her next venture brought her to Midwest, in 1921 oil boom days. Here she worked as a hasher in the Midwest Boarding House. "If you were looking for a man," she said, "this was the place to find one. We served 700 every meal."

Brida worked at this two months, but then came the 4th of July, and the Stampede at Cody. "I told the boss I was quitting because I had a sore toe and that I would not be back to my hashing job, and I rode off for Cody."

"Later I trailed a pack horse carrying my bed-roll and I went on up to Montana, then back to Cheyenne. There was hardly a fence in those days, and I would stop at ranchers' and homesteaders' places to eat my meals. They were always glad for company, and sometimes I'd stay for a few days and lend a hand. I'd feel sorry for some poor housewife with a pack of kids, and I'd

stay and help her catch up on her work."

Brida took to the train to follow the rodeo circuits down through Colorado, and on to Chicago. There she was seriously hurt in a rodeo. "I was bucked of a bronc and I hung up; he drug me around so bad that it hurt me considerable."

Undaunted, she joined up with the *101 Miller's Wild West and Far East Show and Rodeo*. With them she traveled all over. Internal injuries, incurred in the Chicago spill, caught up with her in Georgia, and she underwent near fatal surgery. Homesick and caring to live only to return to Wyoming, she cried and pleaded until she was put on a stretcher and a sleeper train, and was transported to Chicago, Lincoln, and finally to Douglas, Wyoming, hospital. After a time there, she recuperated on the Ogalalla Ranch near her present spread. She lived with Bill and Ethel Whitney until she was well. She told how delighted she was to be back in Wyoming, and said, "You know they don't talk like us in Georgia."

As a single (really widowed) woman of twenty-nine years and lots of experience, Brida homesteaded her place in 1925. Since that time it has always been her home, though for years she followed the rodeos and came home in the off seasons.

She married Roy Gafford in 1926, but later he went his own way and for a number of years, Brida managed her homestead with only the occasional help of haying hands, when she could find some.

The hardest work she recalls was the building of reservoirs. "I used a team and a scoop and got my heels popped off everytime I dumped a load of dirt."

Proudly displaying the two beautifully embossed saddles she had received at Madison Square Garden in New York, Brida said that winning the first World Championship was her life's greatest thrill. "And I'd been scared to death to go to that big town, because I'd heard so many tales about gangsters." That was in 1928 and Brida continued to compete there every year except one from 1928 to 1937. And back in Cheyenne, Wyoming, she won the World's Championship for lady bronc riders. Brida placed in every one of the Madison Square Garden events she entered, and then went for nine consecutive years on down to Boston to place nine times there. She has won in every major lady bronc riding contest in the United States at one time or another.

The toughest bronc to sit was "an ornery critter, called 'Separator'." And Brida confided,

"You know there is a secret to every game you play, and there is a gimmick to bronc riding, too. You want to get the saddle forward, as far as possible, to get away from the back lash. Well, Separator was a sway-backed old bronc, and there was no way to get the saddle forward. I just had to get on without a gimmick and ride on pure nerve. I stuck him out at Madison Square Garden for the World Championship."

Though she did her share of it, Brida hated exhibition riding. She was featured as an attraction on a jumping horse, called "Whiskey." She hated the horse and the jump over a convertible with the top down. And she still stays mad at that Whiskey who gave her a bad spill.

Brida recalls with evident displeasure and distaste some exploitation of riders in early day rodeos in Madison Square Garden. Wily publicity promotors would bait sailors, just off a boat, to do exhibition bronc riding and then set them up for spills that thrilled the crowds no end, but nearly did in the sailors. "The Navy commander found out just in time to keep the navy from being wiped out."

The showmen began luring inexperienced girls onto the broncs for a fee of $25 per ride. They would tie the girls' feet under the horses' belly to keep them on the broncs and Brida was sickened to see one girl beaten into insensibility as her head was dashed forward to the bronc's neck and then back to its rump, until the girl was like a rag doll.

After Brida won her third World Championship in 1937 she decided, "I'd better quit if I want to hold myself together. I had seen too many bronc riders who were all crippled and broke up, and had to beg for a living, and none of that was for me. I wanted to quit while I was winning too, and while I held the World Title."

The only broken bone that Brida had did not come from bronc riding. Her saddle horse stepped in a badger hole and pitched her into the dust—wrist foremost. She said she rode on to her destination of Jackson, and the wrist didn't hurt much until the doctor went to set it, with no ether to give her. She declares that she does not feel pain like most folk do, but she can't explain why.

Retired from rodeos and settled on her ranch, Brida has spent many happy years. There were times however, when things went wrong and she threatened to throw in the sponge and sell out. Times like the winter of '49 when there was danger of starving to death, snowbound on her ranch for weeks. She ate jackrabbits. There was the spring when old Molly's calf died in the late wet snow, and two calves bought to replace it,

took pneumonia and died. Her range cows usually had live calves, though because she stayed with her "ornery cows" until she persuaded them to have babies in the barn instead of on the range.

Brida appears happy as a lark though she has no contact with the outside world except through an antiquated telephone with a private line that runs to the closest ranch and nowhere else. She decided she had best put that in after a sick spell when a hired hand found her face down in the middle of the floor—unconscious. That old rodeo injury had caused adhesions and more surgery was required.

She gets up about 4:30 AM to begin her day, says she "never needs much sleep—six hours is plenty."

For entertainment, Brida has a battery operated radio, and she delights in reading tales of the old Wild West. A favorite magazine is *Frontier Times*, and her excitement about tales of Alaskan ghost towns is catching. She is determined she is going to Alaska and explore some of the old gold mining camps. And she just might. After all, anything *he* can do, Brida has proved she can do, too.

Though selling out would seem reasonable for a woman of Brida's age, and because of the isolation of her place, she always weakens when she remembers spring. Her eyes light up like stars and she says, "I get all tickled inside when spring comes, and the birds are singing and the grass comes green, and the new calves are born."

Pictured Above: Luella Houdesheldt

Velva Mattix
Midwest

Equal Responsibilities

Liberation came a little late for Luella Houde-sheldt, who carried the mail from Casper to the oil field for thirty-one years in rain, snow and mud, as well as sunny weather.

During all those years of accident-free driving, she covered close to a million miles and was the first female driver to be named driver of the month by the Wyoming Trucking Association.

Luella and her late husband, F.W. Houde-sheldt, contracted to carry the mail for Salt Creek Freightways beginning July 1, 1938. Along with the mail, passengers were transported—some of them in a race with the stork.

Among Luella's passengers, there were characters from all walks of life, and sometimes odd combinations turned up that gave Luella cause for concern. For instance, there was the day she transported a genteel, dignified woman along with a noisy Edgerton bar-maid. Sheepherders were often passengers to Casper, and drunks frequently asked for a ride. Luella was in the passenger-hauling business so she had to put up with them.

A ten-year-old boy often put Luella to baby-sitting. The boy's mother worked at a bar and she would send the child to Casper as a passenger in the morning and he would have money with which to treat Luella to the finest dinner in town. He would accompany her as she ran various errands, doing favors for folk out in the oil field. Luella saw to it that he had his hair cut and then delivered him back to Edgerton in the evening.

For a time a regular passenger on Saturdays was a Catholic priest. He rode out with the mail, spent the night in the Midwest Hotel and then conducted Mass on Sunday at the Midwest Community Hall. The priest traveled back to Casper on the bus as Sunday was the mail carrier's one day off.

Luella recalls a time when five male passengers took seats in the car when she got under the wheel, one uneasy rider asked if *she* were going to do the driving!

During those thirty-one years, there was probably never an afternoon that some local citizens were not anxiously awaiting the arrival of the mail from Casper. They were worried for Luella's safety if the weather was bad and the roads were slick. And there were always important messages in the mail bag—letters from lovers, payroll checks, emergency requests for funds from college kids, birth and death announcements. The mail car was Salt Creek's contact with the outside world.

Along with the mail, small freight items were often piled into the car. The items ranged from someone's two front teeth to a corsage for a starry-eyed prom queen. The load for Casper often included dry cleaning and laundry, shoes that needed repair, items to be exchanged for another size, color, shape or style, and five gallon cans of cream.

The mail car was a coupe at one time and this posed a problem with freight, especially the time Luella was asked to deliver an order of fourteen potted poinsettias for Christmas.

In 1957 Mr. Houdesheldt died, and his wife had misgivings about continuing the daily run without his help in bad weather, and his skill in keeping the car in good shape for her. But undaunted, Luella decided to continue and signed another contract for hauling the mail this time with the Post Office Department and the added job of delivering mail to fifty-eight boxes on her route. Many friends were made as she brought the mail to people along the route and Luella remembers with fondness the stops at the John Beaton Ranch. She often had coffee and cookies with Mrs. Beaton in the shadow of Teapot Rock.

Not forgotten are many trips on slick roads and the times of plowing through deep snow drifts—sometimes on the wrong side of the road when that was the only way through. She traveled on courage and hope that there would be no on-coming traffic.

Luella put some 292,000 miles on one of her cars and in 1958 when she won the Wyoming Trucking Award, it was estimated that she had driven the equivalent of sixty-four years of safe driving by the average man, who drives 10,000 miles per year. In recognition of this unusual record, Salt Creek Freightway officials hosted a farewell dinner honoring Mrs. Houdesheldt and presented her with a gift certificate from the firm.

Her last run was on June 30, 1969, and it was without incident until Luella found a farewell card and a box of candy addressed to her and placed in one of those fifty-eight boxes she served. At that, the lady mail carrier exercised her woman's prerogative and cried a little. She was entitled to a few tears for she had proved again—anything *he* can do!

Rights and Responsibilities

ESTHER MORRIS
Photo Courtesy of the Pioneer Museum
Lander, Wyoming

Beryl M. Williams
Casper

Mrs. Esther Morris gave a Tea Party and invited, some say twenty others forty, guests to her tidy miner's shack in the gold mining town of South Pass City. Among these guests were opposing canidates in the pending elections to the first Territorial Legislature, William H. Bright and Herman G. Nickerson, who were influential and interested in the future of Wyoming Territory. During the evening Esther proded the candidates and elicited promises from each of them to introduce a bill which would grant women the right to vote. Bright later won the election and he introduced Senate Bill No. 70.

John Campbell, Wyoming's first Territorial governor smiled as he signed *An Act to Grant to the Women of Wyoming the Right of Suffrage and to Hold Office* at midnight December 10, 1869. Indeed, Governor Campbell signed three addition-al bills protecting and upgrading the status of women. For the first time anywhere in the world women, if widowed, could retain guardianship of their minor children. They could earn and keeep their income; they could hold property in their own name; and they could receive the same salary as men, if equally qualified.

It was no happenstance that bills to protect women's rights became law first in Wyoming; only one-sixth of the population of the newly-organized territory was women. Governor Campbell, William Bright and most of the men of the first legislative session realized Wyoming needed women who would assume their share of responsibility in building the new state. How else could women be induced to exchange the comforts and convenience of the East for this raw land which had so little law and order, so few schools and churches, together with so much isolation and loneliness?

"To the lovely ladies, once our superiors and now our equals," joked some legislators. But it proved to be no joke when Esther Morris was appointed first woman Justice of the Peace and served capably for nearly a year. In March 1870, six women were empaneled on the first mixed jury; they deliberated two days and two nights with Mrs. Martha Symons-Boise Atkinson performing the duties of first woman bailiff.

Justice John H. Howe set standards of courtroom conduct when he addresssed the women saying, "You shall not be driven by sneers, jeers and insults from the temple of justice, as your sisters have from some of the medical colleges of the land. The strong hand of the law shall protect you. It will be a sorry day if any man forgets courtesies due every American lady and paid by every American gentlemen by act or endeavor to deter you from rights which the law has invested in you."

Later Justice Howe said, "The eyes of the world were upon them as pioneers serving in a movement that was to test the power of being able to protect and defend themselves from evils of which women were victims."

Casting off shackles of serfdom and quickly accepting their role, Wyoming women became world leaders: Mrs. Louisa Swain was first woman voter; Mary G. Bellamy was first to be elected to a state legislature; Nellie Tayloe Ross was first woman governor; and Betsy Ross Peters earned the first Ph. D. at the University of Wyoming.

Twenty years after Governor Campbell signed the four bills on the status of women's rights, Wyoming Territory petitioned the U.S. Congress for statehood. By this time, Wyoming men were convinced of the mental equality of women but men of other states were not. Wyoming's delegation encountered stiff opposition over the Female Rights Acts. During the crucial debate women telegraphed, "Drop us if you must. We can trust the men of Wyoming to enfranchise us after our Territory becomes a state." Wyoming representatives replied, "We may stay out of the Union a hundred years but we will come in with our women." Thus, when Wyoming acquired statehood, it was proclaimed the *Equality State*.

And how have Wyoming women used their rights? Almost a century later they still carry their responsibilities. They recognize the power bestowed upon them as a privilege not to be regarded lightly. They vote; hold office; retain guardianship of minor children unless proved unfit; own property; earn and spend their own money as they desire; and in some cases are paid equally to men when qualified. Since 1962 Thrya Thompson has served as Wyoming's Secretary of State, the first woman in the nation to be elected to that position. The heritage of equal rights requires Wyoming women to assume equal responsibilities and they have met the challenge.

First woman jury in the world, 1870, in Cheyenne, Wyo.

Photo Courtesy of the Wyoming State Archives.

Who Stripped the Robes off Wyoming's Goddess of Liberty

Tom Bohnsack
Cheyenne

Buechner design which was attached to the senate enrolled act during the legislative process. It was this design that Chatterton removed before reaching the governor's office.

Chatterton's original nude that caused all the scandal. It was the one that reached the governor with the act.

Grave was the crisis! Mean and comtemptible was the act! She may not have been Wyoming's first streaker, but she was far and away Wyoming's most controversial one. The gal that adorned the design of the Great Seal of Wyoming as signed by Acting Governor Amos W. Barber on January 10, 1891, was more inartistic than lewd, but in that early year of our statehood the general concensus was that she should have kept her beauteous person covered! The uproar continued for months and in the end led to the use of the territorial seal for the first two years of statehood.

Shortly after the first state legislature convened, State Senator Fenimore Chatterton, a Republican from Carbon County, introduced a Senate Joint Resolution calling for the appointment of a joint committee of the house and senate to consider designs for a state seal. The resolution passed and Chatterton was appointed to represent the senate. He was also the chairman. Nat Baker a Democrat from Converse County, and H.E. Buechner, a Democrat from Laramie County served as house members.

Buechner submitted one of the designs considered by the committee and when the vote was taken it was Buechner's design that the committee recommended be adopted.

Chatterton introduced a senate file providing for the adoption of the design. The file passed the senate and the house.

...It was the afternoon of January 10, 1891 that...Chairman Chatterton, author of the act took the enrolled act to Acting Governor Amos Barber for his approval...All was not going well that last day of the first state legislature. The press described the day as a "Tumultous time." Scenes of wild excitement were described in the closing sessions even to the outlines of revolvers showing under legislator's coats.

Chatterton did not become involved in the riotous inclinations of the house. However, his actions that afternoon were to leave him a place in Wyoming's history that is unique. After leaving the house chamber but before reaching the governor's office, Chatterton removed the Buechner design from the enrolled act and attached his own design.

When passed by the legislature, the design had shown a female figure dressed in flowing robes. When signed by the governor the gal...was naked. The design of the Great Seal of the State of Wyoming was just not the proper place in 1891 for a naked lady! At least that is the way Acting Governor Amos Barber felt. When he approved the act, he did so with an exception as to the nudity of the woman. (He later erased this exception.)

It was clear to Chatterton and Barber that the crude design would have to be redrawn and it was agreed that an artist in Rawlins would revise the design and Chatterton would forward it to the governor.

Somehow the new design was delayed so long that other plans were considered.

Complications ensued and the press, not only in Wyoming, but nationally picked up the "scandal" of Wyoming's nude. The Cheyenne Daily Leader described her in most uncomplimentary terms, and Chatterton along with her. The Rawlins Journal tongue-in-cheek came to the aid of the accused, "Senator Chatterton is charged with improvising an undressed female for the state seal. . .Fenimore is altogether too modest to even think of a female in the nude, much less to desire her to be brought before the public as part of the great seal of Wyoming."

The issue made national headlines and while the national press paid very little attention to the facts, they paid a great deal of attention to the scandal. The New York Sun devoted over a column to the story in its editorial page of March 9, 1891. . ."just who the offenders are has not been discovered, but they have been able to do more damage to the reputation of Wyoming in a few days than did all the seal makers of Albany to this state in thirty years." The Sun continued "her beautiful draperies were gone, as if they had been caught in a cyclone. The officers of the state did not notice the change until a number of most important documents, the very title deeds to state existence, were stamped with the highly objectionable seal." Most of the "facts" expressed by the New York Sun simply were not facts. The design was never struck and was never officially used. The Sun was much too pleased with its coverage to let fact intere with the story.

Finally an artist in Philadelphia, Edmund A. Stewardson was engaged to design a seal for Wyoming. By February of 1892, Stewardson had submitted a design to Barber. The acting Governor liked it and instructed the artist to make

Chatterton's revision. It was this design that Chatterton expected Barber to attach to the act.

The design of the Great Seal of the State of Wyoming.

a plaster model. This arrived at the capitol in March 1892, but the governor had other things on his mind that spring. The Johnson County cattle war was on!

The territorial seal continued to be used that summer. Stewardson's design was adopted by the second legislature with one change. The new governor was a sheep man and he asked that the word "cattle" be changed to "livestock." On February 8, 1893 Governor Osborne signed the enrolled act into law and the plaster of paris cast was shipped back to Philadelphia so that dies could be cut. The official seal was first used in the

Secretary of State's office in September 1893 and that instrument is now in the state museum.

Chatterton's original nude design is still attached to the original act and is safely stored in the North vault of the Secretary of State's office.

The official seal of the state of Wyoming looks like the above.

Reprinted from
Cheyenne Sunday Tribune-Eagle
July 20, 1975

The Squirrel Run

Tracy M. Mock
Sheridan

Most
Of the leaves have fallen—
Except for a few
Hardy survivors.
The trees look dark,
Ugly and forbidding.
The squirrels
sense no change,
The trees
Still provide a run.
I see them from my upstairs window.
I guess the difference is
I look for beauty and
My furry friends a pathway
To a black walnut tree.

Lonely Lady

Nancy Curtis
Glendo

Illustration Courtesy of Joan Malone

Laura watched David's pickup turn around the last trailer on the drive. He would be gone until late evening; she was alone again.

She turned on the TV over the crackling of the citizen band radio. The CB radios were David's "toys" and at first she had kept the base station on only to listen for David's voice as he talked to truckers and CBers on the drive to the plant. Lately she'd been keeping it on low volume all day.

Laura straightened the magazines on the Spanish coffee table and picked up TIME.

"Breaker, break," the radio squawked, "how about ya, Bounty Hunter, you got a copy, come on." Laura strained to hear the chatter over the TV.

She dropped the magazine, hit the TV OFF button and moved closer to the CB. A smile turned up the corners of her mouth. Like a country woman on a party line, she was evesdropping on a private conversation. She and David had laughingly talked about the possibility of her doing her master's thesis on the jargon and slang of the CB subculture.

"Go ahead, you got the Bounty Hunter."

"Ol' Country Cadillac here. Anything in those traps?"

Laura recognized the familiar code names of two long-winded CBers, partners in a coyote-trapping venture, she guessed from their talk. Worse habit than watching soap operas, she thought to herself and moved from the radio to empty ashtrays and rinse the coffeepot, as the cacaphony of static and conversation continued in the background.

From the window over the kitchen sink, Laura looked out on the trailers, 180 of them, parked in a vast grey area which differed from the surrounding countryside only because the sagebrush had been stripped, and naked trailers hooked onto the umbilicals of electricity, water, and sewer. There were no lawns, no trees, few skirted trailers; only portable stairsteps, rutted dirt roads, and wind. But they were lucky to find a spot at all in a boom town, David had said. And in the six weeks they'd been there, Laura had seen other families living in tents and out of cars.

The woman from the green Mediterranean trailer got into her car and drove away. She must have a job, Laura thought with a little envy. Her own college degree had opened the door for her only at McDonald's and at the plant as a truck driver. But David had said she didn't need to work, that he made plenty. The price you pay for money was higher than she'd imagined.

The suburban life she had once sneered at—where people raised kids, mowed lawns, and had barbecues seemed tempting now. But this? She felt the moisture overflow her eyes. Roughly, she rubbed it away. She refused to be that sort of person. She would adjust.

The chiming of the bell jerked her head up. My god, first visitor in six weeks and she was tear-stained. She wiped at her eyes again, turned the CB down, and went to the door.

"Hi," the girl said, the wind whipping her brown hair across her face. "I'm Sally Jones with VISTA. We're setting up community recreation activities and wondered if you might be interested in joining our ceramics group?"

"Well, I. . .come on in. Do you have time for a cup of coffee?"

"We'll be giving free lessons in trailer number 114, the silver and blue one over there." The girl ignored the open door. "Every Tuesday from 10 to 4 starting today. You do have to pay for your own supplies. See you? Got it, number 114?"'

The girl swept away before Laura could answer. Ceramics, a bunch of dowdy middle-aged women making ashtrays for Christmas gifts. Laura shook her head in amazement.

She smiled. At least it had broken the monotony. She really ought to go visit her parents for a few days. It might make all this look better.

She turned the CB back up and leafed through TIME. She had already read even the "Medicine section."

"Breaker, break," the voice crackled. "How about a base? One Bounty Hunter here, needing a land line for a 10-5." Laura glanced down at the list of the CB 10-code numbers taped to the side of the radio. 10-5, a relay.

"Bounty Hunter needing a 10-5. Anybody got a copy?"

She had never talked on CB. Somehow she'd always felt too self-conscious to try the jargon which seemed an integral part. Strange, no one was responding. Surely someone else must have his ears on. "Anybody got a copy on this Bounty Hunter?"

Laura picked up the mike and keyed it. "I have a clear copy on you Bounty Hunter, go ahead." Amazing she thought, she sounded almost like one of them.

"I run my pickup in a gully she can't handle. Could you give my buddy a call at 891-6645 and tell him I'm at the trap just north of Jackson Hill? Just need a little nudge to get out."

"891-6645? North of Jackson Hill?"

"10-4, and get back to me."

The telephoned message was taken by a male voice that sounded like Country Cadillac. Laura returned to the base and keyed the mike. "Bounty Hunter, your 10-5 delivered and your buddy is on his way."

"Three's and eight's to you, my friend. What's your handle?"

"Lonely Lady here," Laura heard herself saying. "Glad to be of help." She heard her voice falling into the intonation pattern of the CBers. It had always been interesting, but this was too much. Lonely Lady! Unbelievable, but she had to admit this was the most fun she'd had in weeks.

"Listen, Little Lady, could I buy you a beer some night to settle up?"

"Well, I . . ." Laura felt her cheeks grow hot and then she said in the same pseudo-voice, "How about a drink in an hour at the Ramada?"

"Ooee, Lonely Lady, that sounds like a real big 10-4 on this end. In an hour? This is the ol' Bounty Hunter, all smiles clear here."

The jaunty voice was replaced by a static-y hum. Laura sat very still holding the mike.

The Bounty Hunter. She was sure she'd know

him. Probably dark with hair just long enough to look good with a cowboy hat. Levis, boots, and a four-wheel drive pickup. She'd seen them on the streets, photocopies of the Marlboro Man, with a sheepskin collar pulled up against the wind and a mustache just coving the edges of a cocky grin.

She changed into the blue pantsuit that David called smart-looking; a man like the Bounty Hunter would probably call it sexy. Wonder what his name is, something rugged and abrupt, Bart, maybe, or Mack, or Kirk. Mack sounded right. His hands would be calloused and chapped from the outdoors. Against her softness, they'd feel like sandpaper. She shrugged a shiver from her spine and carefully put on her make-up.

She could hardly believe she was going through with it. She looked into the mirror. Was this really Laura Fields doing this? Lonely Lady smiled back. She patted her hair into place to spite the wind and picked up her coat. It was time to go.

With her hand on the door handle of the car, she stopped. The wind screamed around the trailers. She hesitated, then slowly her hand fell from the handle and she pushed herself into the wind toward the silver and blue trailer, number 114.

At first you were just another summer guest whose Western boots were too new and whose Stetson merely sat on your head instead of slouching comfortably there as did my Dad's and brothers'.

And, as had all the others, you wanted to wash dishes, chop wood, or clean fish. Then, somehow your hat and boots softened, and I no longer laughed to myself over your genteel attempts to belong to this life, my life, here in the Big Horn Mountains of Wyoming where my father "ran" sheep in the summertime. During the winter the sheep were trailed back down to the ranch in the red foothills of the Tensleep country.

I watched as you began to try to plumb my father's depths. You even went down to the ranch with him to pick up supplies for the sheep camps. Too, I saw you carry pitchy logs for my mother's fires.

As for my fires, I wasn't quite sure. But you fed them, too. And on them?

With reflected flames dancing in and out your eyes, I'd feel you watching me and had to turn away. Would the others ever leave? For then you might kiss me and I could be sure. But you only smiled.

We fished Sitting Bull Creek as its sparkling waters flickered and early morning sun began washing willows and gilding grass. Buds with yellow tips popped out, only to bend under our brown boots. We cooked trout for breakfast and laughed over biscuits too brown on the bottom and felt ourselves being taken up into the mountain mystery. Sometimes the mountain was friendly, sometimes not.

Watching a doe and fawn falter at the edge of the meadow, we *had* to ride horseback to the high country and the lakes. I waited for you beyond the shimmering grass, for, of course, you weren't easy with horses. I was wild and loped along the soft wind, letting it lift my hoyden hair.

In the blue piney shade, alone, it seems you'll never come. My horse is straining to get on and tosses his head in protest. Finally now at the end of the trail lies Misty Moon Lake, a huge mirror, black at the edges where pine trees fringe its shores and spread spiked shadows. The middle is a cobalt blue vault, broken into ripples at intervals from trout risings. Together we watch the changing water and laugh with happiness.

There were many places along the trail that day where you could have kissed me—when we sat on the fallen tree trunk at the lake's edge; or, having let the horses drink and rest, we too drank by cupping our hands and letting the cold water trickle down our arms into our shirt sleeves. We never did decide why water lillies grow so peacefully in the ponds and not in Misty Moon.

When sunset too soon turns the water red, we remember that dinner is waiting back at the cabin, and people might worry about us. The horses know that oat bags are waiting for them, and we can scarcely hold them to a walk, especially since it's all down hill, and they know their way.

We were late, and a snapping, roaring fire welcomed us to the hearth. We are terribly hungry, and the shock of many appetites begins to burn in us. A bead of sweat swells and gleams on your forehead, yet you speak only of your dead mother.

After dinner, it rained.

Isn't water supposed to extinguish fire? Not so, not so, and ours is a fiery-wet encounter. You, hearing the staccato drops on the roof, tear outdoors looking for me. I, forever moping under my pine tree, wonder if you have your jacket. We collide just as smoke down-drafts from the stoney chimney at the cabin's corner.

When you take me in your arms and hold me, I shiver, not at the damp night but at the nearness of you and at your kiss. Rain soon soaks your soft, brown hair, causing it to curl and eddy. My shirt

Summer Fire, Autumn Rain

Emilie McKeon Grant
    Casper

looks as if it were poured from a bronze pitcher. In lamp light your face shines with rain drops like huge tears, forming rivulets to flow around your mouth and, inexorably, into mine.

Soft rain whispers and sighs all night, and in the morning as willows quietly wait, the aspen grove quivers and sparkles more than usual.

I hated that September-burned day you left for the city, your eyes lack lustre in the tawny dust of mountain noon. Over in the clearing my bay shook his head and pawed gusts of dust in angry puffs. Your roan, a bluebell dripping from his lips, looked up then stood stockstill watching your car slowly disappear around the bend of the rocky road.

Once I thought you stopped the car, but it went on.

Our horses snorted at the wake of dust while the creek nearby gurgled heedlessly on. When night came, the moon was hidden in the clouds, and the mountain was cold and alien.

Even now I can't endure the sound of rainfall on a cabin roof. Even now when it rains, oh! I taste your salty lips.

A Sweater for the Hired Man

Vandi Moore
Jelm

Photo Courtesy of Mary Alice Gunderson

Old Ned poured the Neatsfoot oil on his ancient boots, rubbing the greasy substance into the weathered folds as if it could, at this late date, preserve their original shine. "If I'm gonna put 'em on a closet shelf, I'm gonna put 'em away clean," he muttered. "I had allus counted on dyin' with them on, not sittin' in a rest home watchin' 'em rot on a shelf. Rest home—humph—takin' me away to a rest home—hell, I ain't tired!"

I had wrestled with the problem of old Ned ever since I married Phil and came to the ranch nearly a year ago. It hadn't been easy to convince Phil he should let him go.

"I don't know how I'll do without him," Phil said. "Why, he was *Dad's* hired man, and he knows the ranch better'n I do."

"That's all the more reason you should let him go. He's getting so old he gets all mixed up."

Like the time last March he left a gate open in the upper pasture and one of the bulls got in with some of our heifers. Phil's a stickler for scheduling his calves, and prefers calving in the spring. Now he was facing calving some time around New Years and he was fit to be tied.

Then in June Phil caught Ned trying to force a heifer to swallow some uterine capsules. "What in hell do you think you're doing, Ned?" he yelled. Later he explained to me that Ned had broken his glasses and couldn't read the labels on the bottles. It was little things like that. And I didn't tell Phil how many times Ned had slipped and called me Miss Marian. A second wife hates to be reminded all the time of her predecessor.

I finally persuaded Phil to go to Cheyenne with me to talk to the administrator at Resthaven. "It may be a few months, Mrs. Barton," she said, "but don't you worry. Some of these old people will pass on soon, and we'll have a place for him."

"Old vulture!" Phil fumed. "Just hovering over them waiting for one to die so she can drag him out and make room for another! I don't think I want Ned put out to pasture on her spread."

I dropped the subject, but awaited word from Resthaven. By the time they had a place for Ned, I 'd have Phil convinced. And Ned, too. I dropped a hint now and then that we were looking for a rest home for him and then when the administrator called a week before Christmas to say it looked like it would be soon, I told him what a nice Christmas present it would be for him—a nice, light, comfortable room, in a home with lots of other people his age, and with his own TV set where he could watch all the cowboy movies he'd like.

"Shucks, Miss Gretchen," he objected, "I'd ruther be ropin' my own calves than watchin' somebody do it on the idiot box." But he polished his boots, took his Ace Reid cowboy cartoons off the bunk-house walls, and folded his extra pair of levis to pack in his cardboard suitcase along with the sweater he said Miss Marian knit him the first year she was on the ranch. The sweater was almost worn out, he said wistfully.

I didn't have time to knit sweaters for the hired man. I was too busy learning the business of ranching. I hadn't got a degree at the University for nothing. I was going to put Phil's spread on a paying business even if it meant me helping him myself with the branding and the roundup, and even the calving. Everybody makes such a fuss over calving. Why, ever since time began, cows have had calves. I couldn't see why all the fuss.

The only thing Phil hadn't quite forgiven Ned for was letting the bull in with the heifers. He was dreading the calving and hated to miss the stock show in Denver because of it.

I've never been to a stock show, but the women around here all look forward to it, and I guess I would, too. I get sort of a kick out of wearing my tight whipcord pants and fringed leather jacket. Phil says I fill them out in all the right places. Oh well, we'll go to the stock show next year. Ned won't be around to let the bull in with the heifers in the spring.

While Phil was in Laramie one day the employment agency sent us Tex. I had dropped in a week earlier to see if they might have any ranch hands available. I wasn't dumb enough to think that Phil could get along without *someone*.

Ned sort of got his nose out of joint when Tex moved in, and when Phil came home he hit the ceiling. "When I want to hire help, I'll hire them!" he shouted at me. Then I cried and said I just thought I was being helpful, and he apologized. "I'll let Tex stay through Christmas, he decided, "but then he has to move on." I knew he wouldn't let him go then, because by that time Ned would be at Resthaven, but I waited for a better time to tell Phil.

I thought we'd drive Ned over to Cheyenne after dinner on Christmas Day. The administrator said they'd have entertainment that night and it would be a good time for him to come. When it started to snow early on Christmas Eve, I remembered we hadn't put the new snow tires on the wagon. Phil went over to Harmony in the afternoon to have them put on.

Ned was polishing his boots when Tex came in from the Barn. "There's a heifer up there actin' sort strange, Ned," Tex said. "Looks like maybe she's gonna drop her calf early. She'd better not! Mrs. Barton said I could go in to Laramie tonight for the Christmas Eve dance."

Ned put on his boots and went to the barn. By this time you couldn't see the bunkhouse for the storm, much less the barn. I told Tex he'd better head for town in the pickup, and beat the storm in. He didn't lose any time starting.

Phil came in right after dark. "Lord, it's rough out there," he said. "It took me an hour to drive the two miles from Harmony."

"Goodness," I said, "I hope Tex won't have trouble in the pickup!"

"You let him start out in *this*? Good Lord, Gretchen! All the roads in to Laramie have been closed since four o'clock! I'll have to go in the jeep to find him."

I was feeling pretty miserable by ten o'clock. Christmas Eve and my husband was out in a blizzard looking for a hired man. He took two thermoses of coffee and plenty of blankets. "If I get stuck pulling him out, we'll spend the night in the pickup," he said as he pecked my cheek and left.

Ned came in for a cup of coffee. "Where's Phil?" he asked. "I'm afraid I'm going to need him."

I told him. "Can't I help?" I asked. Other ranch wives talked about helping pull calves. This would be a good time for me to learn.

We picked our way through the storm, hanging onto a rope Ned had strung from the barn. The snow whipped our faces and I stumbled twice. Ned helped me up and finally we stepped inside the barn. A light hung low over a calving pen where the heifer was secured. I gasped. A long, awkward leg protruded from the animal's swollen backside.

"The other foot's caught inside," Ned said. "We've got to work fast or we'll lose both the heifer and the calf."

I thought for a minute I was going to faint, then I summoned courage to ask, "What shall I do?"

"Get the calf puller."

"The calf puller?"

Ned didn't look up. He was busy pulling a long plastic glove and sleeve over his right hand up to his shoulder. "Look in the bin by the door. You'll find a big plastic sack with an instrument in it. Bring it to me."

I found the bag and when I returned I thought I was going to vomit. There stood Ned, his arm rammed clear inside that cow's backside and he was twisting it around and the cow was making a low moaning sound. "What are you *doing* to that cow?" I asked indignantly.

"I'm turning the calf's other back leg, Miss Gretchen. It's twisted in there and I couldn't pull the calf." Suddenly he drew out his arm, all covered with a slimy mess, and in his hand was the calf's other foot. He reached for the bag I held, took out the instrument and fitted it quickly on the heifer's back and rump, fastened a cable to the calf's feet and began slowly to crank a reel. The calf's legs moved a little, then a little more, and then as the cow strained against her pain, a little spotted face appeared behind the legs and suddenly the cow ejected the rest of the calf.

I stood there transfixed. What I had just done was to watch the miracle of birth, in a stable, on Christmas Eve. And the old man who had pulled the calf stood there beside me, a young triumphant look on his face. I saw then what I had not seen before. Ned needed to be needed, and life for him would never be finished as long as he could participate in the miracle of it.

Somehow I helped him clean up the calf and when we left the barn it was standing awkward and soft and velvety beside its mother. Outside, the blizzard had stopped, the clouds had parted, and a hazy moon hung over the barn. I didn't even mind when Ned took my hand and said, "Here, Miss Marian—let me help you—"

The jeep stood by the kitchen door. Phil and Tex had just come in. "I found him stuck in a drift four miles up the road," Phil said. "I had a devil of a time getting the pickup out, then it slid off again, so we just left it there."

"Nobody's likely to bother it," I said. "Then the day after Christmas you and Ned can take the jeep and go pull it in while I take Tex to town. He'll want to be at the employment office early, and I want to pick up some yarn. I'm going to knit a sweater."

It was the end of summer. The highway that had teemed with tourists' cars the past few months stretched almost deserted now, in front of the weathered wooden building set carelessly down in the middle of a vast and empty rangeland.

POLLY'S PLACE, SPEEDY ONE-STOP SERVICE was outlined in flickering neon above the sagging roof of the porch overhang, and there was a neatly lettered sign above the door, UNITED STATES POST OFFICE, PRAIRIEVILLE, WYOMING. Three gasoline pumps painted in bright red and royal blue made a splotch of color against the dun-beige landscape of cured grass and sere sagebrush.

Two people sat on the rough wooden bench in front of the store. The sun was setting and long rose-colored streaks of light burnished the tanned arms of the fifteen-year-old boy and put a momentary flush on the sallow cheeks of the old woman. They sat together silently, searching for words to say to one another as they waited for the east-bound bus to come.

It was Lester's last day at Polly's Place. School was starting the next day and he was going back to town on the bus to rejoin his family and start his second year of highschool.

"You're crazy to go out there to work at Prairieville," his friends had told him last spring. "Nobody around but that old woman. Man, you'll be out of your skull by fall. It'll be dull, really weird."

He smiled now in the red sunset light. What an exciting summer it had been! She had made everything fun, even silly little things that a guy wouldn't have thought could be interesting. But they were.

The End of Summer

Betty Evenson
Casper/Hiland

Photo Courtesy of Archie Nash

There was the day he discovered the chipmunk nest under the hood of Polly's new car. The little baby creatures running in every direction went through the vents into the car so that Lester had to take the vacuum cleaner hose and poke it into every niche of the inside of the car before Polly would get in it.

They worked crossword puzzles together, poring over the dictionary and a beat-up encyclopedia that Polly had found in the old schoolhouse before it was torn down. And one week they got on a State capitals kick with the tourists' cars that stopped for gas, and if Lester got the most correct he could have an extra serving of dessert for dinner.

There was Jeopardy on TV in the mornings but this was usually interrupted by customers just as a Daily Double came up. And the project of finding out which presidents' pictures were on all the bills—Polly had to call the bank in Casper to find out about the fifty and hundred dollar ones, since they didn't get many of that denomination at Polly's Place.

He supposed Polly was old; she must be because she could remember when there were coal stoves and Model T Fords and oranges came packed in wooden boxes. But Lester never thought of her as being any particular age. She was interested in all the same things he was, and she laughed a lot.

The sun sank below the rim of the prairie and a sharp north wind sprang up, bringing with it the smell of smoldering garbage from the incinerator behind the store. Lester stood up.

"I'd better get some water and put on that...thought the fire was out, but there must have been some old papers underneath that are still burning."

He loped away on long, strong legs. Polly turned to watch him go.

Her friends had said at the beginning of summer, "Why do you want to get such a young kid to work for you? He won't take any responsibility. You know how kids are; you'll have to tell him what to do over and over each day."

She smiled remembering incidents. "Lester, do you think you could climb up and put a light bulb in the overhead sign, I noticed a few days ago, it was out." "Yes, ma'am, I noticed it too, I put a new bulb in yesterday."

"Lester, today is the fifteenth, would you take the old magazines off the rack for me, so I can send back the covers?" "Oh, I did that while you were watching television; I cut off the covers and listed them here ready for you to mail. When I

wasn't busy this morning, I read the meter for the electricity, and don't forget this is the week you're supposed to make out your post office report."

Lester came back from the incinerator, his brown eyes gentle. "The rabbits came to say good-bye to me," he said, speaking very low. "And those two antelope we saw last night are out beyond the fence."

"It's been such a short summer," Polly said, her vigorous voice which was young like her eyes contradicting the heavy arthritic movements of her large body as she stood up to stretch her back. "Seems like only yesterday you came to work."

"Yeah," Lester answered. They both sat down again on the bench.

"She's sure to be cranky and bossy, too. Bet you won't be able to do anything to please her," Lester recalled one of his friends saying. Now he remembered Polly's voice, excited and happy the day he borrowed a post-hole digger from the Thompson ranch and fixed the gate-post in the side yard that was about to fall down. "Wow! You couldn't have done anything that would make me any happier!"

He thought of the time somebody had ordered eight double-dip icecream cones while he was servicing a car out front. He came in washed his hands and took the dipper away from Polly. "Here, you collect for the gas, he'll be in a minute. This vanilla is so hard, you'll break your wrists!" She had smiled at him—a smile that made him feel good all day.

The rising wind blew bits of paper and debris through the air. Polly flinched as a piece of flattened Russian thistle scooted around the corner of the building, low to the ground and alive looking. "I thought it was a salamander running!" she gasped.

A trucker hauling oil field equipment went by, blowing his horn and waving to the two on the bench.

"Too bad we didn't get a car from Rhode Island," Polly said, shivering in the cool wind and pulling up her apron to cover fat red arms. "Every state but that one!"

"Yeah, even Alaska and Hawaii."

The sun was down. Twilight spread an inky stain across the landscape. Lester looked at his watch. "Bus is late."

"Van's relieving Red and he's always late," Polly answered, "He can't keep a schedule to save his neck."

There was a long silence. The sound of the truck shifting gears on the big hill half-a-mile away came to them faintly.

"When you get back home, Lester, won't it be nice to sit down to eat a meal without being interrupted by that darned buzzer from the gas pumps?"

Lester did not answer.

"And I'm sure your mother will do a more imaginative job of cooking. I'll bet you're so sick of boiled potatoes, you never want to see another one."

Lester turned his head away and swallowed hard. "I like boiled potatoes," he said gruffly.

He liked the way it had been at suppertime, just the two of them, too tired to talk much. Plain food, hot and plentiful, and Polly always smiling, even when she had to put their plates back into the oven several times while they waited on customers.

The bus came into view along the highway with its turn signal blinking. Neither said anything, and they sat without moving until the bus stopped in front of the building with a loud puff of air brakes. Lester reached down then to pick up the piece of blown tumbleweed and tossed it into the litter barrel beside the front door and grinned, "So much for your salamander!"

Van didn't let the passengers off the bus, because he was already late. Polly gave Van the pass slip and Lester picked up his brown paper sack of clothes. In the doorway, Polly touched his arm, "I'm going to miss you, Lester."

He looked full at her then for the first time during the evening. "Goodbye," he choked and then smiled.

The bus roared away leaving a trail of diesel fumes on the pure evening air. Polly stood alone beneath the neon sign, watching and waving until the bus was only a tiny speck in the wide loneliness of the prairie twilight.

Illustration Courtesy of Chip Wood

Rancher-Racer Ben Moore, Casper, Wyoming
Photo by: Beryl M. Williams

Emperor Nero and 180,000 Romans cheered charioteers to victory and then for centuries Rome's splendid play-days with the Chariot Races at Circus Maximus vanished into the mists of history. Not until the 1920's in the tiny Thayne, Wyoming, was Chariot Racing reborn in a very different way. It spread throughout the Rocky Mountains, and is rapidly growing into a new sport across the country. Twentieth century Chariot Racing still tests the skill and stamina of man against man, horse against horse, and both against nature in its surliest mood.

Snowbound and isolated from early fall through late spring, Thayne ranchers and townspeople needed respite from boredom of long winters in Star Valley, south of the Grand Teton Mountains. When they finished evening chores, men raced each other on horse-drawn bobsleds down Main Street, while townspeople lined both sides of the street shouting for favorites to win. Racers were evenly matched, as nearly as possible, and losers paid the orchestra for Saturday night's dance.

Like a winter blizzard, racing enthusiasm spread through Star Valley to nearby Jackson and

Chariot Racing Reborn

Beryl Williams
Casper

Afton, Wyoming as well as Driggs, Idaho. Soon communities throughout the Rocky Mountains were challenging each other. The first three inter-community races were held at Thayne. In 1948, the All American Cutter Racing Association was organized after cutter (sleighs with runners) replaced bobsleds. Because of Jackson's larger population and tourist fame, annual competition was designated to be held there on Washington's birthday, February 22. Hundreds of spectators struggled across pine-capped mountain passes, drifted deep with snow, in sub-zero weather to watch.

No Roman ever bedecked his chariot more flamboyantly than rancher-racers. You could see ranchers painting and adding fancy decorations to the body of their sleighs and honing runners knife sharp to glide more swiftly across crusted snow. You could hear them repairing harness and brushing horses in barns. Most picturesque of all was the rancher-racer bundled in heavy woolens, high-buckled overshoes, gloves, cap and ear-muffs.

From the beginning, any man who could drive a team of horses was eligible but it took more to win a race. Winners developed an uncanny knowledge of chariots, harnesses, and especially of horses. Drivers learned the strength and weakness of their teams, and competitors' teams. If one horse pulls either left or right, the owners put blinders on it; if a horse is high strung and nervous, they stroke it gently and soothe it with words softly spoken. Men exercise their horses daily. A driver's allegiance is totally to his team.

No one can change a racer's mind if he prefers Quarter Horses, he always selects them because Quarter Horses are noted for fast starts. Those who think Thoroughbreds are best stick to that kind. Still others prefer a mixture, breeding Quarter Horse to about one-half or seven-eighths Thoroughbred, since they believe that horses with pure blood lines don't reach maximum speed until the short quarter-mile race is about over.

Who could predict whimsical winter weather? Tracks, swept bare by high winds, were glare ice. Or, cutter runners mired deep into muddy tracks. Or, cutters looked ridiculous on dry tracks. No snow—no cutter races. Resourceful ranchers salvaged car wheels and axles and added them to chariot bodies. From then on, they rode in either cutters with runners or chariots with wheels, depending upon the weather . . .

Rome copied its races from Greece. Allegedly in 680 B.C. Greek charioteers robed in white and sleeveless chitons raced two-horse teams, and

Photo Courtesy of Beryl Williams

later four-horse teams, near Olympia. Their gruelling twelve laps around a rough circular course completed was eight miles. Rome shortened the distance to five miles but increased hazards. One by one charioteers paraded before the emperor and his retinue. Then pomp ended. Wine and weather warmed the Romans, "*Vae Victus* (woe to the vanquished)" they shouted. Charioteers' whips lashed out to their own teams, to other teams, and onto competitors. Charioteers rushed for leads, sharply cutting in ahead and throwing opposing teams off stride. Broken chariots, injured horses, and maimed drivers were scattered around the elliptical arena at Circus Maximus by day's end. Often only the victor finished the race. . .

Copying the Romans, today's charioteers parade well-groomed teams and flashy chariots before judges and hot-dog-munching throngs to the starting gate. A split second after teams enter the gate, they break into a 440 yard race toward the finish line. Danger and disappointment and defeat—or *Winner's Luck*—begin at the starting gate. For example: Sometimes chariots are jerked fifteen feet; if they fail to land right side up, chariot and driver are dragged until the horses are stopped. Sometimes when gates open, nervous horses paw the air, hesitating, and losing fifty yards in seconds. Sometimes driverless teams, reins cracking like a cat-o'-nine-tails, zigzag down the track while the erstwhile driver dodges oncoming hoofs from the ground where he was thrown by the forward thrust of his team. Yet the crowds shriek when they think they see a loser; but instead, a driver and his team suddenly spurt into the lead to win.

Chariot racing has come full circle since Rome's holidays from bobsleds, to sleighs, and back around to chariots again. You'll never see a modern charioteer robed in a white and sleeveless chiton; he will probably wear a Stetson hat, Levis, and cowboy boots. There is no more winter boredom for rancher-racer. Nearly every weekend they load three horses (a pair and a spare) into trailers, pile chariots into pickups, and haul them to one town or another to race two fast horses down quarter-mile straightaways in a rebirth of this ancient sport.

Return of the Buffalo

Archie Nash
Sheridan

Buffalo are returning to Wyoming—not in the huge herds that once surged like dark shadows across the prairie, but in small privately owned herds scattered across this sprawling land.

While Wyoming is known as the "Cowboy State," it is the figure of a buffalo that is prominently displayed on the state flag and emblazoned on the sides of the Highway Patrol cars.

Rightly so, for before the coming of the white man, the area that was to become Wyoming was the vortex of the countless herds moving in their circular migration routes. South Pass, then hardly known to the white man was the principle passage the shaggy beasts had for their east and west movements across the Rocky Mountains in what is now Wyoming.

Dotting the rangeland as far as the eye could see, the "Indian cattle," besides supplying the needs of the wandering red men, provided food for the dust-stirring emigrant trains and the hungry crews building the Union Pacific railroad. Then came the great slaughter of the 1860's and 70's. In an incredibly short time, the countless numbers of this native animal were virtually wiped from the land.

As strange as it may seem today, the elimination of the buffalo was regretted by few white men—certainly not the cattle owners coveting the rich, waving grasses, the settlers wanting to plant the fertile land, or the business people catering to the new comers. The killing was encouraged by the United States government, so that the hostile Indians would be forced to surrender because of starvation—accomplishing a feat which the army had failed to do in all its years in the field.

The buffalo and the plains Indian will always be linked together by romanticists. While at one time buffalo ranged over most of the North American continent and Indians lived from coast to coast, it was the Indian hunters dashing on horseback among the thundering herds that captured the imaginations of the historians and writers of the west. Much of this romanticism exists today and likely is a major factor is the establishment of the domestic herds in Wyoming.

Certainly the state, itself, has done little to encourage the buffalo industry within its boundaries. For years it has taxed bison on the same basis as cattle. Recently Wyoming refused the donation of a private herd, labeling them as domestic animals. But the state has now given its blessing to a small herd maintained in the Hot Springs State Park at Thermopolis, Wyoming. Roads winding through the pasture land enable the visitors to see the great creatures close at hand.

Private enterprise has placed the buffalo or America bison, as they are known to the naturalist, on the tax rolls of thirteen Wyoming counties, with the numbers increasing each year. Some counties have listed but one. By far the greatest number is accounted for in Campbell County where over 2,000 head are maintained by one large operator.

The demand for buffalo meat far exceeds the supply and is an attraction for restaurants fortunate enough to be able to include it on their menus.

Buffalo raisers contend that grain fed buffalo are leaner and tastier than beef and practically devoid of cholesterol; that it can be eaten by many with high blood pressure without ill effect.

Another stimulus in buffalo raising is the current craze to cross buffalo with cattle, hoping to acquire crossbreds that inherit the buffalo's freedom from many of the illnesses which plague cattle; require less care with the ability to stand cold; and increase their gainability in feed lots. Not reaching sexual maturity until three years of age, there is no need for castration. Buffalo life span ranges from twenty to forty years.

Domestication of the buffalo is dispelling the misconception that buffalo are ferocious animals. Temperamental, yes, but not nearly as dangerous as they have been pictured over the years. Those raised in small bunches and handled properly cause no great problems. Most breeders have learned to work the buffalo with pickup trucks, motorcycles, and on foot. Horses are picturesque, but generally not satisfactory in handling these huge creatures as they are usually afraid of the buffalo and the buffalo are not of them.

It is when buffalo are closely confined as in corrals or trucks that trouble starts. The larger animals have a tendency to hook the younger buffalos, often throwing them high in the air. At that time the buffalo will charge over man or rider without hesitation.

The young calves are red in color and with their undeveloped hump resemble a slightly deformed red angus calf. As they grow older their color darkens until at weaning time, they are almost as dark as their mothers. When very young they are extremely curious and will readily stagger over to an observer. Their mothers take a dim view of this and so should sightseers.

One author writing about buffalo, said in effect, "Buffalo cows are notoriously poor mothers, practically abandoning their young. This is why so many calves die of starvation or fall victim to predators." Nothing could be farther from the truth. There are few animals that the offspring and mother remain in such close proximity as a cow buffalo and her calf.

Buffalo breeders have also learned that once the animals are properly located in a pasture, much of the trouble of keeping them home is eliminated. Contrary to popular belief, buffalo do not have tendency to crash fences, except when fighting, but prefer to jump them. A good five-foot high fence usually suffices.

These days buffalo meat is more likely to be found simmering in the modern kitchen of a white man or sizzling on a barbecue grill in his backyard than bubbling in the smoke blackened pots of his red brother.

To truly appreciate these fascinating animals and the aura of romance they are bringing to Wyoming with their return, an effort should be made to see them through the eyes of the red man. Because of the tremendous part the buffalo played in the tribal life of the early day Indian, the western history student cannot but wonder if the "Great Spirit" did create the mighty buffalo herds just for the Indian alone, as all the old Indians of the plains-dwelling tribes so firmly believed.

These "Indian cattle" supplied their every need from cradle to shroud. It is doubtful if Nature ever blessed any other race by providing all the necessities and luxuries in one animal that required no care or attention from the people it fed, clothed and sheltered. To the plains Indian this animal was such a blessing, and with the passing of the buffalo went the glory and power of the red man in his wilderness existence.

The rewards of the buffalo hunt were like leaves on the tree there were so many. The huge shaggy robes were sewn together to fashion the coverings for the comfortable conical tepees which were so precious to the Indian because they were home-loving people for all their roving nature. The tanned robes with the long wool made soft beds that defied the icy blasts of the winter storms.

The softened skins were made into the Indian cradle with its stiff back in which the youngster could be slung on the mother's shoulders, hung in a tree where the breezes whispered lullabies, or stood up in the tepee by a dancing firelight. And when a member of the tribe had gone on the last long journey to "the happy hunting grounds" his body was carefully wrapped in the best of buffalo robes and placed in a tree or on a high scaffold where it would be unmolested except by the elements.

Tribes ranging along the larger streams too deep to ford stretched tough old bull hides over a frame-work to form the curious round coracles or bull-boats. These boats which resembled huge shallow bowls were very buoyant.

The long wool-like hair scarped from the robes was used in stuffing their pillows and saddle seats.

The dried buffalo manure or "chips" were universally used by the plains Indians for fuel. It was the prairie "charcoal," for it made considerable heat without much smoke to betray the camper's presence to his enemies or to frighten away game.

Old and young alike were nourished by the rich red buffalo meat. It was the Indian's principal article of food and many times their only one.

From the broad sinew in the loins came their bow strings and thread. The tallow seasoned the cooking, salved their sores, and served as the base for their war paints.

The whitened skins became handsome garments under the skilled fingers of the squaws. Beaded tobacco pouches, moccasins, tables, floor coverings, bags to hold the owners' "medicine" and all small possessions, or bags for dried meats and berries. . .all were made from buffalo hide. From this same animal also came the Indian's saddle cover, quivers, shields for protection, lariats, throngs and hundreds of other everyday necessities and even luxuries. The symbolic

Photo Courtesy of Archie Nash

writings on tanned skins became their historical documents.

From the bones were made handy camp tools, hide scrapers, and ornaments. The horns became cups and soup dishes. The buffalo carcass even supplied the tanning material for its own hide. After the hide had been scraped free of grease, it would be liberally smeared with a tanning mixture made by mashing boiled liver and the raw brains of the animal together. The hide, after receiving this coating, was worked over a sharp edge until it became soft and leathery.

With so many blessings coming from one animal, it was no wonder that Indians considered the buffalo an especial favor from the Great Spirit for his red children.

The annals of the West contain ample proof of the contentions of the tribal sages. How different might the stirring chapters of the early frontier read if the white buffalo hide-hunters and cattle-men had not exterminated the huge bison herds in so short a time. Another angle of interest to the military-minded man would be a conjecture on how long it would have taken the crack troops of the United States army to catch and subdue the wiley warriors of the plains if the buffalo had remained plentiful.

There is no doubt that the Indians' way of life was doomed with the discovery of America. It was only a question of time until he would be cornered and ground under the merciless heels of civilization. Even so, it would have taken many more years for the blundering white soldiers to have chastised the red men into submission if the valleys of their hunting grounds had still been dotted with grazing buffalo. Hunger and lack of wild game more than once forced the elusive plains-dwellers to come within striking distance of the white soldiers. It was not the armies under Generals Miles, Terry, Reno, and Custer that defeated the warriors and the great western chiefs, though not one bit of glory should be taken away from the achievements of the white troops, but it was the selfish efforts of the hide-hunters and grass-craving stockmen.

Because life and the buffalo were virtually the same to the nomads of the American plains, the shaggy animals played a major part in all their religious ceremonies, too. Dried buffalo tongues tasted in the Sun Dance, the most sacred of all ceremonies to the Indian, were used as the sacrament in their rites, much as wine and bread is used in the communion services of Christians. The sundancers dragged around huge heads of freshly killed buffalo until the leather thongs were torn through the shoulder muscles to which the thongs were attached.

It seems fitting in the scheme of things, that an Indian should have made the first attempt to preserve and domesticate the buffalo so the once vast herds would not suffer total extinction. Samuel Walking Coyote, a Flathead Indian was far-sighted enough to try and his success is his sole claim to fame. Ironical as it may seem, Walking Coyote died later from the effects of a spree after receiving $2,000 as his share of the proceeds from the sale of buffalo to the Canadian government in 1910.

This Flathead Indian and his family were on a hunting expedition in the Milk River county in 1873 at the time the buffalo were being slaughtered in such shocking numbers. While the family was there, six little orphan buffalo calves, whose mothers had been killed by hunters, wandered close to Samuel's camp. They were captured and cared for by members of the family. Most of the work fell to Joseph Ahtati, the small step-son of Walking Coyote. The hard trip back to the family's home at the junction of Mission Creek and Flathead River, Montana, took the lives of two of the buffalo calvs. The surviving four, two bulls and two heifers, were kept picketed close to the cabin. Later when they were large, Joseph herded them in the hills nearby.

The descendents of this small nucleus have supplied many of the buffalo in the national parks and the impressive herd of over 10,000 animals that now range in the large preserves of Alberta, Canada.

From Canada and from the increase in other small remnants of the original herds that were protected to individuals in the United States, come the present day herds, which are growing each year.

Once more the great shaggy buffalo is at home in Wyoming.

A Prehistoric Bison Hunt

William Bragg
Casper

Some hunters of gem-like projectile points and other artifacts look all their lives for just one *Paleo-Indian point hoping it will be perfect! When the Egolff and Laird couples, who were arrowhead hunting, found a fluted projectile point near the newly constructed Control Data computer plant near Casper, they immediately placed that information in responsible hands.*

Dr. George C. Frison arrived soon and determined that this could possibly be a site worth excavating. The problem was that the site was right next to a plant parking lot, and less than fifty yards away was the constant stream of highway traffic on Interstate 25. Besides, the site overlooked Casper, a city with over 40,000 people living in it, a far cry from the situation that existed when those projectile points were left there.

It could have happened this way:

The ancient hunters clutched stone weapons at their sides listening to the big herd of buffalo across the river. They waited patiently for the animals to cross the North Platte, but they couldn't see them. Fog and mist rising from the river obscured their view.

The hunters waited silently. They knew the herd would follow the trail which led from the river bottom to the area they had chosen to trap and kill the buffalo.

These hunters had watched the herd the night before and saw several old bull buffalo, the leaders, cross the river and bed down for the night. The hunters knew then that the rest of the herd would follow these leaders across the river the next morning.

That was when they had selected their kill site. A well worn trail led into a long, narrow sand dune filled with deep sandy soil. When the buffalo herd moved through this dune, the hunters planned to rise up and begin the kill. The heavy sand would slow the big beasts down. When they tried to climb up and out of the trap, the hunters would send their spears against them.

The women, children, and old ones waited in the rear. They carried old hides, heavy now with spears and hammerstones and skinning tools. When the kill started, those in the rear would rush up and join the hunters helping to form a ring around the trap.

This would be a vital kill. Soon the sky would fill with snow and the rivers would freeze. Now was the time the people would have to find their cliff caves and prepare to outlast the long winter. The meat and hides won here today would provide food and cover until the green grass replaced the winter once more.

Several young scouts slipped back to their stations. This indicated that the herd was on the move. The wind hadn't shifted, but came steadily into their faces. That was good. No smell of man would excite the herd turning them away at the last moment.

Now, the chug-chugging of the labored breathing of the big buffalo was carried to their ears on the morning breeze. That noise came from deep within the barrels of the big animals' chests, as they climbed slowly up the steep river terrace to the grassfields hiding the hunters and their sand trap.

As the morning breeze parted the ground fog, the shaggy brutes emerged from the grey shreds of fog, and filed slowly into the trap. The hunters held their breath, waiting for just the right moment to spring the trap.

Now! The hunt leader rose. He shouted and threw his spear into the side of a fat cow buffalo. The rest of the hunters followed suit, each picking out a good target and sticking his spear into it.

The women, children, and old ones rushed up to join the hunters and handed out more spears and hammerstones to the hardworking men. Everyone was shouting and yelling in the excitement and the buffalo were bellowing as the kill progressed and the strong hunters knocked down the buffalo who were frantically trying to climb the wall of the trap to safety.

The kill was all over in a few minutes. The exhausted hunters sank to their haunches as they watched the women and children and even the old ones slide down into the sand dune. Then they joined them, and the job of butchering the successful kill began. There would be food and shelter for the winter months.

Archeologist George C. Frison led an archeological dig on the outskirts of Casper in May and June, 1971. He was assisted by graduate or undergraduate college students who were either interested in or majoring in anthropology. Cooperating, too, were the owners of the land and adjoining land, the state, county and city officials. Deep in the bed of an ancient sand dune, sixty projectile points were found among the fossil remains of over 100 now extinct bison. The site was dated with a radio carbon test at 10,000 years before the present time.

Reprinted from WYOMING'S WEALTH by permission of author and the publisher, Big Horn Books, Basin, Wyoming.

Mammoth Glacier, the source for the Green River. Photo Credit: U.S. Geological Survey

Wyoming's Glaciers

Ann Gorzalka
Big Horn

Wonderful Wyoming, the Cowboy State, synonymous with Yellowstone Park, Cheyenne Frontier Days and Indians.

But glaciers? Yes, according to the U.S. National Geological Survey, Wyoming has approximately eighty glaciers.

They range in size from the small ones found in the Big Horn, Teton, and Absaraka Mountains to the big ones in the southern part of the state. There in the Wind River Range are some sixty glaciers. Seven of them comprise the largest ice fields in the United States, except for Alaska, and have a total glacial area one-and-one-half times as great as all other Rocky Mountain glaciers combined. These seven are located on both sides of the Continental Divide and waters from them eventually reach both the Atlantic and the Pacific.

The seven big glaciers can all be contained in a rectangle nine miles long and five miles wide.

The largest of the seven is Gannett Glacier. It has an area of 1,130 acres and is located east of the Divide and north of Gannett Peak.

Mammoth Glacier, north and west of Gannett Peak, has a glacial area of 990 acres. It is often referred to as the Green River Glacier because it is the largest of several ice fields which form the head-waters of the Green River.

Sacajawea, third in size of the Wind River seven, has a total area of 940 acres. The glacier is located between Mt. Helen and Mt. Sacajawea in Fremont County. Knife Point Glacier is on the east slope of the Continental Divide and extends southeast from Fremont Peak to Knife Point Mountain. This fourth largest of the seven studied by the Geological Survey Team contains 740 acres and extends over two-and-a-half miles in its longest dimension.

Dinwoody, 660 acres and fifth in size is separated from Gannett Glacier by the small Gooseneck Glacier. This ice field is the most accessible and, therefore, the most often visited. Dinwoody Glacier measures two miles by one-and-a-half. Fremont Glacier lies on a broad high shelf south of Sacajawea Glacier and has a total area of 1.03 square miles which includes the two almost separate parts—upper and lower Fremont. It is classified as a tandem cirque glacier.

The most northerly and smallest of the seven is Helen which lies betwen Mt. Helen and Mt. Warren and spreads east for about one-and-a-half miles.

Smaller glaciers in the Wind River Range beside Gooseneck with its 87 acres are Minor, 214 acres; Baby, 100 acres; Heap Steep, 45 acres; and Twins, 143 acres. These small ones are cirque glaciers.

Mammoth, Helen, Sacajawea, and Knife Point are valley glaciers. Gannett and Dinwoody are palmate cirque glaciers and Fremont is a tandem cirque.

About three-fourths of all the fresh water in the world is stored as glacier ice and a close watch is kept on all glaciers. They are photographed and measured at frequent intervals because they indicate what is happening to the climate. The effect of glacial retreat or advance on stream flow has important consequences for long-range water resource planning. Whenever runoff is less than precipitation, water in the form of ice is added to storage, so the glaciers grow and advance. When water is released from this storage and runoff exceeds precipitation, glaciers retreat.

The estimated July-August streamflow from Wyoming's eighty glaciers is thirty-five billions of gallons of water. One billion gallons would cover over three thousand acres of land to a depth of one foot, or would fill 91,000 standard railway cars making a train 900 miles long.

Wyoming with its colorful past, its coal-and-oil-rich present can consider her glaciers as another valuable resource to be measured in dollars as well as gallons for her enviroment, people and industry.

Glacier at foot of Cloud Peak, Big Horn Mountains looking west-northwest. This glacier is in Johnson County. Photo credit: N.H. Darton

Credit for research:

U.S. Geological Survey, Denver, Colorado, and Washington, DC
Dr. M.F. Meier's Master Thesis
World Data Center a Glaciology, Tacoma, Washington
Visual Services, Geological Survey, Reston, Virginia

Photo Courtesy of Richard Kerwood

The Mountain Climbing Man

Jake Brouwer
Sheridan

People sometimes talked about David Levi and laughed behind his back. I rarely did, because I was his friend. Some referred to him as a braggart, a show-off, and too loud. He managed somehow to be the center of attention in any group. Because he was sensitive to the sham and materialism of modern life, he often was caustic and critical. He had an avid interest in contemporary affairs. David berated politicians. I thought his outlook was too cynical. His education had been in European schools. In 1939 he fled Europe because of Hitler's growing power. He kept seeing events in America heading toward the same bitter culmination. Those he talked to either acquiesced silently or they took issue and got into a heated argument.

David was a worshipper of the body, his body mostly. He was an excellent mountain climber. I cultivated his friendship because, to me, he was a fascinating personality and following him was a way to get out and into the mountains. He told of scaling many of the prominent Alpine peaks. While working for his Masters degree in Colorado he conquered most of the over-10,000 feet summits. David was a born teacher, very exact and definite with information, and dictatorial in his demands on subordinates.

He gave opinions freely. "Kids these days are flabby, because they're lazy. You've got to work at it, to keep in top condition. Most people overeat, and watch sports rather than participate." It was David's theory that once you started to hike, resting too often was bad for the heart. An easy steady pace was best.

Tishe was David's wife, the companion of his many adventures. They complemented each other. He used her, while she, more subtly, used him too. When there was disagreement in the party, and David's ego got ruffled, she built him up again. I got to know Tishe well, mainly from our hikes. David liked to spend most of his time with the younger hikers, concentrating on the females. So Tishe and I would find ourselves ahead of the leader and his lagging students. Other times it was reversed when David and the competitive youngsters raced ahead to gain the top of a peak or to be the first one to see a lake. At the end of a day-long adventure, there would be a contest to see who could be back at camp first. David usually proclaimed that he wasn't in the least tired, and some of us would laugh.

Every summer David, Tishe, and I organized an ascent on Cloud Peak, the 13,000 foot monarch crowning the Big Horn range. The climb wasn't hazardous, but a worthy effort that tested young and old alike. For me it was an annual test of my strength and virility, proof that I wasn't failing yet. David scoffed at the idea that age could cut one down. He kept himself at a fine edge of fitness, so that few could guess he was over fifty.

This year's climb, like others before, was a glorious exhausting struggle through grassy, flower-sprinkled fields sloping, at first gradually, then abruptly, up to the summit. We sloshed through icy streams tumbling from high snow banks, jumped boulder to boulder, wormed our way through narrow gorges cut by running water and winds. Increasingly often we leaned against giant granite slabs to catch our breath.

Not surprisingly, Tishe and I found ourselves isolated from the youngsters and David. The top was still hours away. I didn't try to keep up with them. For a time David's sharp high-pitched shouting sounded ahead followed by the laughing answers from the young climbers. Soon they melted into the wind sounds. Tishe and I kept laboring up the trail, watching for cairns which thoughtful earlier climbers had placed to mark the way. Our pack sacks were weighted with sleeping bags and a day's supply of food. We all planned to sleep on top this night.

Tishe jabbered pleasantly. We were old friends and had been in similar situations before. There was beauty in the clear sky, in the rocky panorama of ridges now above the tree line. I felt the exhilarations of movement. The rock-chucks were scolding from lookout points above. An eagle was pivoting distantly in space. From time to time I gasped for oxygen in the rarified altitude, and nausea gripped me. As we struggled upward on the sharply chiselled boulders, I had a tendency to lose my balance; this worried me.

Tishe showed concern as the hours ticked by with no sign of the others. We stopped to rest and to scan our horizon. No movement up or down the trail, only rocks and dwarfed trees and the sound of running water splashing down the mountainside.

"I'm sure they're all right. David knows these mountains. They're probably already at the peak, making camp."

I laughed at her. She worshipped David, her Superman. "He probably took the wrong trail, and got lost," I chided.

"Oh! no, not David. He'll be waiting for us on top, wait and see." We pushed on. Tishe was in good shape—better than I.

She is not bad to look at, I thought—somewhat stocky, with a good strong round face, and a well-proportioned body. A nice girl—I concluded—and a good wife for David. I wondered if part of her tenseness now could be that we were alone on this cold beautiful mountain.

Abruptly Tishe turned to me from above. "Did you hear that shot?" She appeared anxious. "That's David. He wants to tell us where he is."

I hadn't heard a shot but chose not to contest Tishe's pronouncement. David, I knew, sometimes carried a revolver on hikes to shoot at rabbits or, as he liked to say, for self-protection. I hadn't remembered that he took one this trip.

There were no more shots. The grinding exertion of the day climaxed as we pulled our weary bodies up the last of seemingly interminable ridges. The apex, a hugh chunk of upthrust granite stuck into a still blue but darkening sky. Obscure light rays filtered through blood-red clouds besmirching the West.

Tishe and I sought out some level areas to spread our sleeping bags. For a pillow I rolled my boots in my canvas jacket. Out of deference for Tishe I upzipped my bag and worked my aching body, fully clothed, into the warm interior.

Tishe was chattering, optimistically, "David and the kids will be here any minute now. They can't be far behind us."

The night was bright, and the stars close overhead. They were diamonds glittering. The air became increasingly chill. There was little to say. My bag heated and I dozed off.

"Listen, did you year that?" Tishe broke the stillness.

"No, what was it?"

"David, he is shooting again...funny you didn't hear it."

"Well, maybe so, but I hope they get here soon." The soft warmth of my bag was lulling me to sleep.

It was going through my head, vaguely, that Tishe long ago had told me David would kill her if he ever found her with another man. Slumber blotted out further thoughts of Tishe lying in the bag next to me. Despite a bone-weary body, sleep came only fitfully. The thin down filling gave uneven protection from roots and rocks that protruded into my flesh. Squirming for a comfortable position, I wondered if Tishe was thinking of the shots and what they might mean.

Long hours later, close to morning it seemed, a noisy commotion jarred the night's stillness. David and his exhausted young hikers had found us. They were disputing loudly.

"This is the damndest, lousiest hike I've ever been on," a disgruntled eighteen-year-old shouted as he flung his bag to the ground and threw himself on top of it.

"He kept telling us we weren't lost. Like hell we weren't."

"What a nightmare that was," cried a girl's shrill voice.

David's sharp retort silenced further protests. "Oh, come on now. You softies can't take it. We had a nice time today. Sure, we took a shortcut once in a while to look at the scenery better and to take in points of interest. But lost? No sir, we were never lost." Then like a kindly father, he ordered them to bed.

"Now all crawl into the sacks and to sleep. And no more of that silly talk. Tomorrow will come soon enough. We'll get up at daybreak, make an early start. That way we can walk the ice-crust on the snow bank before the sun melts them and we sink down to our crotches. We'll have a nice hike down to Lake Solitude and catch our limit of trout before dinner."

Tishe was relieved to have everyone reunited; I could tell.

"We heard you shooting when we were down on the trail," she smiled at David.

I caught a glimpse of his sharply chiselled face in the faint moonlight as he looked up from unzipping his sleeping bag. "It must have been somebody else you heard. I don't have a gun."

Some of the youngsters were already snoring, and peace settled on the mountain top. As I dozed off again, it perplexed me vaguely how Tishe could have heard those shots so distinctly.

The next morning during our descent from the chill heights of the peak, David and I were together, resting briefly. I accosted my friend in a joking tone. "How come, David, you never admit when you make a mistake? Last night, for instance. You know damn well you guys were lost."

"What a ridiculous statement," his sharp reply came with quickening irritation. "These young people came on the trip to see the mountains. I walked them along, taking our time, to observe the rock formations, to explain the topography. We stopped to see birds, interesting flora and the insect life at these high altitudes. It makes no sense to just rush up the trail with your eyes closed." This last, I knew, was meant for me.

It worried me, sometimes, that David rarely stayed on the trail. He was forever taking shortcuts which would take him miles into the wilderness, down some narrow canyon, or over a nearly impassable gorge. Friends he had hiked with often had humorous anecdotes about his "shortcuts."

Almost a year after that memorable climb to Cloud Peak, I was home alone on a holiday—Labor Day—and was restless. I drove an hour to the Tongue River Campground not certain how far I'd walk up the canyon. It was a cool bright day. Dry seed-pods hung over the trail. The poison-ivy leaves were a sober red, and far away on the mountains, aspen groves were turning. A melancholy mood smote me in the wild picturesque canyon. My thoughts were preoccupied with David, who was no longer with us. He had plunged to his death on the Box Canyon floor one day last spring, just about three miles ahead of where I now was. His life had been wrenched from him violently when he tumbled down a steep embankment of loose shale and then pitched headlong over a sheer wall one-hundred feet to the unyielding stone riverbed below.

David had been restless to get into the wilderness. He had called several friends, all of whom had other plans, so he ventured out alone. Tishe worried and warned him against going.

At parting he assured her, "Don't you worry. I've been up there many times. I'll probably be back early tonight."

Well, he didn't come back. She waited with

growing anxiety. Finally she called a friend, who hurriedly assembled a party of eight men to look for David in the Boxes. I was one of them. It so happened that by taking a shortcut through a tangle of roots and rocks, I was ahead of the others that spring day. It was then that I saw David, life-like from a distance, kneeling as though he were drinking head down on the rocks alongside the forked Tongue River. One boot was dangling in a cold little rill of the divided stream. Coming closer, I knew that life was gone. The top of his skull was crushed; a nasty bruise marked his face. The others hurried up. We carried him with all the care and love we felt for our friend—through the twisting riverbed trail to the waiting horses and thus to an ambulance at the campground.

So today as I hiked up the trail alongside the noisy Tongue, David kept coming into my thoughts. This, to me, is now David's Canyon, I thought—someone should see to it that the name is changed. He loved this lonely primitive spot, despite its rattlesnakes, its poison-ivy and its treacherous rock walls. . .I kept thinking about him.

Along the river-bank darted a little bird, called a dipper. It disappeared into the water, stayed submerged for about thirty seconds and then reappeared some ten feet away scampering over the wet rocks in search of insects.

I walked on braced by the cool morning air, saddened by reflections about David and the day last spring when his friends struggled to bring him out of the almost inaccessible Box Canyon. The steep walls lay before me now, partially hidden by trees and the ascending mountain slopes. The trail had taken me high above the river, so now to reach the canyon floor I had to leave it and make my own way. The running water looked to be a half-mile below. The steep walls into the Lower Box appeared impossible to descend, but on closer inspection there were footholds and passages down past rocks and trees and brush. "Better take it easy," I cautioned myself. "Don't do anything foolish." I was feeling strong and confident, probably the same way that David was last spring.

As I carefully lowered myself into the canyon depths, shadows from the sheer walls cast gloom over what had moments before been a sparkling day. At the water's edge there was no trail—only wet boulders and a profusion of vegetation blocking the way. At one point I snaked my body through a natural bridge carved by the swift waters rather than exhaust myself muscling up over a bluff. Finally, there was no path but up. Testing every tuft of grass or brush before trusting my weight to it, I climbed on. My progress was halted by an overhanging ledge with

Photo Courtesy of Richard Kerwald

a smooth top a foot or two above arm's reach. No crevices for hand holds.

"Well, I've got to stop for breath a minute anyway. This is sure a tough climb. I wonder if this is still David's trail?" He was, I mused, no doubt looking for another good fishing hole, working himself up-river. Then I glanced to my right and detected some tackle and a fish pole sprawled in a clump of vegetation. The cork of the pole had been eaten into by forest creatures. I tucked the pole under my arm. Then turning and looking over my shoulder to the left, I suddenly recognized the river broken up into many streamlets and rushing over a smooth stone bed. It was the place where we had found David last spring.

"Good God!" I breathed awestruck, "This is the spot."

One section of the fishing pole was missing, and I wondered if it were up on top of that shelf. Maybe David had found a way up. I looked for holds in the smooth rock, but could find only a crevice tantalizingly beyond my reach. David was shorter than I. Maybe by jumping he could have got a grip on it...It's possible he decided to try for it, lost his hold, and fell backward...I reasoned. It seemed important to figure out what had happened.

Then, surveying the sharply sloping hillside of loose shale to my left, I spied a shiny yellow nylon rope dangling down in the direction of the canyon wall. The top end was looped around an uprooted bush.

I shuddered...looks like he gave up on the ledge, tried to get out by roping a bush, and the whole thing pulled out of the ground...methodical thoughts went through my head as I tried to reconstruct the tragedy. I could see David, the proud skillful conquerer of Alpine peaks, taking this last chance. He tried one more alternate route—hardly a shortcut, to get over one more ridge. Then the frantic moment when...clutching for anything to arrest his fall, he plunged to the rocks below.

From ahead of me now came sounds of waterfalls thundering and below the blue streamlets appeared far away. A brief spell of dizziness came over me. There was a feeling of panic when I realized how far I'd come. I had been caught up, almost trapped, into replaying the final moments of David's life.

"This is a crazy thing to do." I said to myself. "I'm going to get out of here and fast, without taking any more chances."

Carefully I retraced my way downward, ever so cautious, taking no risks. It was as though I had spent one last day climbing with my friend, David, and I was relieved to be hiking back down the trail.

93

4:20 Sunday   January 13, 1973—

It was the last run of the day, and I wished it would never end. The sun had poured like drawn butter over the mountains all that afternoon, and a good foot of powder snow had fallen the night before, offering an irresistible invitation to skiers of all ages and abilities. I was feeling particularly buoyant about the way I had taken the runs considering I had just come through the beginners' instruction class. I set my edges parallel down the hill and let myself sail into the wind, a free spirit, barely skimming the earth. Like a kid, I wished I could ski on and on, forever downhill.

But the lift line had closed behind me on my way up, so I knew it was over for the day and that there might not be another day so splendid the rest of the season.

As I neared the bottom of the hill, I sensed an urgency in the air. A couple of ski patrolmen were loading toboggans into the pickup camper which served as an ambulance to the ski area. I caught bits of information:

"Leek's Canyon..."
"Two people—a kid, I think—"
"—Avalanche!"
"...volunteers—fast as you can—"

Photo Courtesy of U.S. Forest Service

Snow Rescue

M.W. Hoffman
Jackson

Well, this wasn't exactly the kind of extra skiing I had hope for, but I'd sure volunteer.

"I wanna help," I yelled to one of the patrolmen who was hurrying the last of the supplies into the camper.

"Go to Betty's," was all he said.

Fortunately, I knew what he meant; I had been at Betty's during a hunting spree the previous fall. It was a roadside coffee shop on the highway near the mouth of Leek's Canyon, on the other side of the designated ski area. One could take the chairlift up Snow King Mountain and ski down the back side through the canyon to the highway. Besides providing a longer route, the powder skiing is unparalleled. I wondered, though, what anybody was doing going down that canyon today what with the little orange DANGER CLOSED AVALANCHE signs posted in warning all along the top of the ridge.

I debated whether to go home and put on extra clothes. I decided against it in favor of time. Besides, the day had been so warm and beautiful. At 4:45 I pulled into Betty's small parking lot, now overflowing. I put my skis on and hurried to join a line of workers who were ready to embark. It was easy to spot the man in charge. He was a big man who moved with authority, whose grey-white sideburns defied the confines of his hood. He handed me a first aid belt.

"Any experience?" he asked gruffly.

"No, but—"

"Fall in beside Ernie—and leave your poles."

His attitude momentarily unnerved me. I was, after all, a volunteer—I was not trying out for a position on his team.

I located Ernie with little trouble. He wore the rust-colored ski patrol parka and had his name in bold letters on the front.

"Who's the wheel," I asked.

Ernie smiled. "Everyone calls him the Snow Ranger," he said. "You're better off to listen close to every word he says—he knows avalanche rescue inside and out."

"Still," I objected, "he could be nice about it."

Ernie sighed. "Well, this is risky business and one hell of a job. I guess he's pulled too many dead people out in his day. And there's the responsibility of safety for all the rescuers—it's not an easy job."

We had formed a short line of about 20 men and were the first team to leave for the avalanche area. The Snow Ranger led the way. Ernie carried a shovel; four of the men wielded toboggans; a few had backpacks and miscellaneous gear. The day had been mild, but now as we started the gradual climb toward the mountains, the sun was setting in a spray of fading pink and the temperature fell with each upward step. A wind heralded the approaching darkness, capricious at first, then strong and bitter cold as we leaned into its force. I wished I'd worn more clothes. I pulled my collar up over my ears and curled and uncurled my fingers and toes in an attempt to lure back some warmth.

In the last faint light of day, we approached the avalanche area. In the greying of twilight it looked gruesome and ugly. Terror seized me at the thought of two real flesh-and-blood people—people a lot like me—trapped somewhere beneath all that. It appeared that both sides of the canyon had slid at once forming deep boulders of snow in the gulley between and fanning out toward the bottom where the land leveled off. If the people could have made it another 600 yards, they would have been out of all danger. We stopped in a small group of pine trees below and to the right of the slide area, left our skis, toboggans, and other gear we wouldn't be needing right away. The Snow Ranger sent Ernie and a couple of other patrolmen to make a hasty search of the slide. Probe poles were passed around and a red nylon cord was tied around every waist for ease in locating any of us in the event of another avalanche.

"The avalanche danger was high today," began the Snow Ranger in his gruff, impersonal way. "We still have an extreme danger from sloughing cornices." He motioned to the heavy jagged edges that were left hanging in the air, where the first slides had broken away. "We do have temperature more in our favor now—but this wind is bad. Now, who hasn't probed before?" Two of us raised our hands. "OK," he said, watch the others. Probe first at your left toe—then at your right toe. Move ahead about a foot, and probe again. Foot by foot. Thoroughly, but gently. There is always the chance of striking the victim's face. If you feel *anything*, tell the shovelers and they'll dig, but you keep on probing. Questions? OK. John and Paul, you be our lookouts. They'll watch those cornices from a safe vantage point and if something looks suspicious, they'll yell—and you run. We should have more teams here any time now. We have a wide area at the bottom, and a deep area in the middle to search so let's get going. Ernie and the others came back reporting no sign of clothing, equipment, or anything to indicate a shallow burial.

We waded awkwardly through the hip-deep snow to the toe of the slide. Huge slabs of snow, harder than concrete lay before us. We helped each other up—fourteen probers, two shovel bearers, two men on the string which would move ahead of the probers, straight and sure. John and Paul were some distance away, below us. Twenty strong we were—and yet like pindots upon the vast landscape. I didn't see how anybody could possibly be alive under these tons of ice, even if they were buried superficially. We began our probing, inch after inch, minute after minute, hour upon hour. Occasionally someone would cry "Object"—and hopes would rise— and the shovelers would dig, but all that turned up were stumps or tree limbs or sometimes a disguised earthy knoll.

Darkness had washed over us—black and cold. The night wind whined in protest. At first the men had talked a little with each other, but soon there was nothing more to say. My feet and hands had long since grown almost numb. The headlamps worn by a few of the men threw grotesque shadows into the canyon. Finally, a sliver of moon found its way over the edge of the hill to shed a timid light upon the snow. A second team of rescuers came and began their procedure below and to the left of us. They had brought food and coffee and started a warming fire in the trees. We were given a short break from our probing. Stiff with cold, I floundered to the fire and folded my fingers gratefully around a cup of hot coffee. Toes and fingers ached and burned alternately.

"Think we'll find anybody alive?" I asked, wolfing a sandwich.

Ernie replied, "Can't ever tell. Some people make it for several hours. Others it suffocates within a few minutes. A lot depends on how they land—if they're hurt, or if they are lucky enough to have their face in a sizeable air pocket. I kind of think a lot of them die from sheer fright, or shock."

"It seems," I ventured, "that a person could make an air pocket with his hands."

Another fellow, directly across the fire, who was beating the air with his arms to get warm, shook his head, "Survivors say that just as soon as the slide stops moving, it hardens into steel. The way you land—that's the way you are." He stopped for a bite of sandwich. "Then you can't tell if you're up or down, and it's pitch black."

Ernie said, "The pressure, or weight, is so great against your body you can't expand you lungs very easily—even if you've got the air to breathe."

It was making me sick. "It sounds ghastly," I said. "Do you know who we are looking for?"

"A man," said Ernie, "a Mr. Hadley and his

nine-year-old son. They're from back East, out here vacationing. Guess he went down Leek's Canyon last year and thought it was great skiing.''

"But why would *anybody* go past all those 'closed' signs on top?'' I wondered. They were posted like beads on a necklace.

Ernie shrugged. "Everybody thinks it can't happen to him. This feathery snow looks so harmless.''

It was true. It did. "But,'' I put in, "if I had a little boy like that with me, I sure wouldn't take the chance.''

A little warmer and more awake, we returned to our probing. A third team had come and begun at the toe of the extreme left of the area. Victims, I learned, were usually found at the toe or near the toe of a slide, at varying depths, of course. They could "swim" an avalanche with much success if their paraphernalia didn't drag them down— which it usually did. Some people had been ground through an avalanche and thrown to the top, or near the surface, it its very last roll. One man had been buried for seventy-two hours and then found alive. There were lots of strange tales about this little-known mystery of nature.

My extremities returned to their half-frozen condition. My joints stiffened and my mind wandered aimlessly through the realms of semi-consciousness, the way it does when one is driving hour after hour into the night. Sometimes the cry "Object" would rouse me to my senses and other times the wind would quit its monotonous whipping and would regain some alertness, but mostly it was just: left toe, probe, push, easy. . .hard spot. . .push. . .a little harder. . .there. . .deeper. . .something? No. . .no. . .push. . .God my feet are cold. . .up. . .right toe, push, push. . .harder. . .easy. . .I could eat a horse about now. . .down . . .down. . .down. . .

I had lost all track of time. We were nearing the upper extreme of the avalanche now. We were looking up the sheer icy cliff to the jagged slabs that hung heavy about us. Shadows magnified their treachery. They were about three feet thick and had nothing but maybe God holding them. All the first team were sluggish with fatigue and dulled by the howling relentless cold. How long into the night would we go?

Suddenly I was jarred awake by a strong, strange feeling. I didn't know what it was I felt, but it was like a premonition that something was going to happen. Instinctively I prepared my body to spring for the safety of the trees. With my adrenalin running at full throttle, I scanned the cornices leering above me. I listened intently but all I could hear was my heartbeat in my ears. Had the wind stopped? Maybe that was all it was. No. A sense of uneasiness had spread down the line as though we were all on the same electric current. We looked from one to the other expectantly for the answer. Maybe it was the warning. I had often woundered if people, before they died or were killed, had some kind of warning, some extrasensory thing. Perhaps they had ignored it, or like us, didn't know what to do about it. Was it a whimper I heard? My ears searched the night, straining above the internal throbbing of my fear. Yes, it was a whimper—but where? Others heard it. It came from far away. . .then it came from the snow beneath my feet. . .then it was behind. . .then above. Everyone turned this way and that in blind confusion. Something was happening. But what? what?

Then we saw it. To our far left, toward the top third of the avalanche, above the third team, an old hunched woman, clad only in a dress and shawl, was clawing in the snow. Beside her, digging and whimpering and wagging his tail was a huge grey dog, or wolf. Before any of us could think, the Snow Ranger had grabbed a shovel and was scrambling over the ice boulders. Others followed pell mell. By the time I got there, the diggers had dug about three feet down had uncovered a knee—a small sized knee. From the position of the knee, we knew the head was uphill and face-up. Carefully then, the snow was removed from the left arm which lay protectingly over the face. The one doctor in the group crowded in anxiously to inspect the boy. We all held our breaths, oh, if only—if only the boy could be alive . . .

"No ice mask,'' the doctor said quickly. As he lifted an eyelid and shined the flashlight into the pupil, we heard a faint groan. The doctor immediately prepared him for mouth to mouth respiration. Someone else ran with the rescusitator. Others renewed their efforts in probing and digging in the area around us. One of the diggers turned up a ski tip. Minutes later the boy's father was found in spread eagle position, head-down face-up. Blood from his nose and mouth masked his face. Light rigor mortis had set in. The doctor pronounced him dead and he was bundled onto the waiting toboggan. A small group of dedicated men had gathered around the boy, waiting a chance to help wherever they could. The Snow Ranger, big and gruff as he was, spoke gently and reassuringly to the boy as he made the child warm and comfortable as he possibly could. The doctor said he was breathing normally then and the boy began to talk a little. No one wanted to say it, but you could feel that everyone was glad it was the boy who was alive.

As suddenly as it had begun it was over. My watch said 11:00 o'clock. The few of us who were left began gathering the remaining supplies and breaking camp.

"Hey," I asked, "Where did that old woman come from—and where did she go?" There had been so much excitement and suspense, I had forgotten about her until that moment.

The others stopped what they were doing and gave me strange, long looks.

"What'd I say?" I queried again.

Ernie spoke up. "You know that is the first time I ever saw her for myself. Been hearing about the old Mountain Woman and her wolf hound for years. I've heard she only appears when someone is still alive."

The Snow Ranger cut in. He seemed in much better spirits now. "Remember last year when the little three-year-old boy was lost from his parent's camp? Spring of the year—all the rivers were high. He was gone for—what—about thirty-six hours. Had every posse in the country out looking.

The kid shows up in camp around suppertime—said an old lady and her nice dog found him by the river bank and brought him back."

"Hey—wait a minute" I interrupted, "what is she—a ghost or something?"

The Snow Ranger shook his head. "Can't be." he said, "Nobody believes in ghosts."

"Some of the old timers around here can tell you some good stories about her," Ernie went on, "Guess she's been roaming these hills for the last fifty years or so."

When we got to Betty's, we received word that the boy was going to be all right. Knowing that made the whole night worthwhile. Even the weariness drained from my bones.

As I drove back to town, the twinkling facade of neon welcomed me to the real world. Houses and pine trees along the quiet streets wore big airy fluffs of new snow. Everything was peace. I remembered making snowflakes out of paper when I was a boy and decorating the schoolhouse windows with them. I wondered if I would ever again think of snow without remembering an old hunched woman, clad only in a dress and shawl, clawing at a drift, a grey wolf-dog by her side.

The Year Devil's Tower Hit the Headlines

Jerre Jones
Casper

Wyoming is the only place on earth it could have happened, and once was enough, apparently.

Because the tall, lonely monolith of stone known as Devil's Tower is the only one of its kind, it stands to reason that it had to be challenged sooner or later by a parachutist.

That's what brought a daring young man named George Hopkins to Wyoming back in 1941—to prove it could be done. And braving the freakish winds that swirl around the top of the venerable old natural skyscraper was only half the battle. Hopkins had to face equally chilly blasts from the startled National Parks Department, which takes a dim view of anyone suspected of trifling with the dignity of a National Monument such as Devil's Tower.

But it was the difficulty encountered in getting

the title-holding parachutist off the Tower which finally riveted the attention of the entire nation on his daring feat, and on Devil's Tower itself.

Never before or since have so many people all at one time been enthralled by the geology, the mythology and the history of Devil's Tower, as writers and photographers from around the nation converged on the remote area for the six days it took to get Hopkins safely back to civilization.

Even the stiff-necked opposition of the Parks Department relented somewhat during Hopkins' ordeal, as some officials realized the overall impact of the publicity being generated for the nation's first National Monument.

Off the beaten track, even to the present day, the volcanic uplift is in the northeast corner of Wyoming, and is usually associated with the Black Hills of South Dakota and Wyoming.

It was, in fact, in the tourist mecca of Rapid City that the Devil's Tower caper was conceived, and it was indeed a publicity-oriented plan, intended to call attention to a Jaycee-sponsored air fair scheduled later on, at which Hopkins intended to try for another world record to pin to his parachute.

At the time of his historic Devil's Tower jump Hopkins held two U.S. parachuting records—total number of jumps (2347) and jumping from the greatest height (26,400 feet). He also held the world's record at that time for the longest delayed jump (20,800 feet).

He brought with him to the Devil's Tower jump, at the age of 29, an impressive wealth of experience in stunt flying and jumping for Hollywood movie studios, plus a couple of year's service training pilots in China and parachutists in England before the U.S. entered World War II.

The fall of 1941 was the lull before the U.S. would be plunged into the war. Slightly more than two months before Pearl Harbor—on October 1—Hopkins took off with his pilot, Joe Quinn, from a hay field a few miles from the Tower.

According to his own description of the event, Hopkins used only one chute for the jump, reasoning that an emergency chute might tangle with the main one in the erratic winds and cause him trouble.

He jumped from the plane at 1200 feet above the Tower, and about 1500 feet south, having calculated the wind drift ahead of time. He was counting on a huge rock in the center to stop him from being dragged off the edge of the Tower after landing. Hopkins said as he approached his landing he realized he was going to overshoot his

target, so he partially collapsed his chute to correct the situation. This caused him to land harder, skinning his ankle, but he was almost exactly on target, the chute on one side of the rock and himself pulled tight against the other side by the wind.

Release of the news to national news services later that day of Hopkins' unprecedented antic was a welcome alternative to the constant and worrisome war news which had dominated front pages those days.

What no one knew at that point was that Hopkins would have to spend nearly a week on top of that isolated pillar, with rats, chipmunks and birds as his only companions, waiting as various plans of escape were initiated to rescue him. Even the children of the Sioux and Kiowa Indian legends were not required to stay long on top of Devil's Tower, as the great bears which clawed the vertical ridges in the rock were summarily dispatched.

The most spectacular effort to rescue the parachutist was launched by the Omaha *World Tribune*, which arranged for the Goodyear Blimp *Reliance* to be sent form Akron, Ohio, to pick up the stranded jumper in a special pick-up basket. Because of inclement weather, the blimp never made it closer to Wyoming than Omaha.

Earl Brockelsby, youthful owner of the Rapid City Reptile Gardens and one of the original planners, along with Hopkins, of the Devil's Tower drop, had intended for the stunt man to lower himself down the side of the Tower by using a rope and pulley arrangement. Brockelsby had arranged for Quinn to return to the Tower as soon as possible and drop the necessary equipment to Hopkins so he could lower himself to the foot of the 865 foot pillar before darkness set in. In fact, Robert Dean of Rapid City Radio Station KOTA, another of the original planners, asked Brockelsby to be sure Hopkins didn't get down too fast or he would not have time to release the story before it was already outdated.

The first drop of equipment was unsuccessful, however. The pulley, the axle and the sledge hammer to be used for anchoring the rope, stayed on top of the 300 by 600 foot area, but the tightly-coiled rope bounced like a ball and disappeared over the edge of the Tower. Time was lost before Hopkins was able to make it known, through shouts and signals to the people beginning to gather at the base of the Tower, that his rope had fallen out of his reach. Pilot Quinn had landed at Rapid City and left the airport before it was known the plan had gone awry, and another pilot, Clyde Ice, was procured to make the next drop. The second coil of rope was dropped loosely, to allow it to splash instead of bounce, but this again proved unsuccessful because the result was a tangle which Hopkins was unable to unravel.

At this point, with darkness nearing, it became apparent that Hopkins would spend the night on the Tower, so a drop of food, extra clothing and blankets was made to help him through the chilly October night.

The ensuing days and nights became a continous nightmare for those trying to get Hopkins down from the Tower, as it became evident that he was not going to be able to lower himself as planned. In spite of the fact that he was marooned in a highly unprecedented situation, with half the world scratching its head over how to get him down, Hopkins never panicked nor complained, but let his would-be rescuers know with notes dropped over the edge that above all he did not want anyone else's life endangered in the attempt to rescue him.

During his six-day vigil Hopkins experienced several stormy cold nights, with rain, sleet, ice and fog, but his spirits remained remarkably buoyant, according to reports of those keeping in contact with him during those days.

Brockelsby had become convinced, meanwhile, that a mountain climbing group from the east coast, which had been one of the first to scale the Tower using mountaineering techniques, was the most likely candidate for rescuing Hopkins.

He contacted Jack Durrance, then a medical student at Dartmouth College in New Hampshire. Durrance was founder and president of the Dartmouth Mountaineering Club, and had climbed Devil's Tower two years previous to Hopkins' drop, after spending several days figuring out the exact route he would take to the top.

Durrance agreed to fly to Wyoming, and to bring his own climbing partner, Merrill McLane. Brockelsby was footing the bill for the various expenses involved in the affair, using money he had set aside to buy his own home, he later reported.

Another principal in the cast was Newell Joyner, head custodian of the National Monument, who appeared early in the scenario, almost concurrent with the arrival of Hopkins to the top of the Tower, and was understandably concerned with the outcome of the affair.

By the second day, Joyner had called the Rocky Mountain National Park headquarters in Colora-

do, and two experienced ranger mountaineers were sent to Wyoming to attempt to scale the Tower. Ernest K. Field and Warren Gorrell, Jr., started up the morning of the third day that Hopkins sat atop the rock, but after climbing about 150 feet, one of the men slipped and was injured slightly, and they returned to the bottom. They recommended calling the more experienced Durrance and his party.

Up to this point Joyner had been highly annoyed with the whole affair, telling Brockelsby he expected dire repercussions from the Department after Hopkins was finally down, but his feelings changed when he received a call from the Area Park Supervisor at Omaha. Joyner was advised of the Goodyear Blimp which was on its way west, and was told to keep Hopkins on top of the Tower until it got there because the Park Department "liked the publicity angle."

Durrance and party were already on their way by this time, however, and had not the blimp been weathered in at Omaha, the parachutist might have spent an even longer time waiting for a decision on who was to have the privilege of rescuing him. As it turned out, Durrance was forced to make the trip by train because the weather was too bad for conventional flights as well as blimps.

Meanwhile, as the world and Hopkins waited for Durrance and company to perform the final rescue, a variety of other suggestions were considered, including trying the experimental autogyro, a forerunner of today's helicopter. Also promoted by Radio Station WOW in Omaha was the use of a Coast Guard amphibian plane equipped with a special gun to shoot a line that could reach the top of the Tower, and down which Hopkins could slide in a breeches buoy. Hopkins temporarily considered jumping off the edge with his chute, but decided the sloping edge of the Tower would make it impossible.

Wyoming's mountaineer Paul Petzoldt also offered to help in the rescue, and drove from Jackson Hole through an early autumn blizzard to join the Durrance party. Then a climbing instructor in Teton National Park, and later the founder of the National Outdoor Leadership Training School in Lander, Petzoldt turned out to be the climber selected to belay Hopkins down the side of the Tower when the time came, because of his strength and his experience in teaching beginners.

The rapidly worsening weather conditions caused much concern, as ice began to form along the sides of the Tower's vertical columns during the fifth day. By midnight Durrance and party arrived at the Tower, after flights from Denver and Cheyenne were cancelled by weather. They arrived with police escort and sirens, and were met by the Colorado and Wyoming mountaineers to begin an early morning assault on the Tower to rescue Hopkins.

The sixth day of Hopkin's stay on the Tower was on a Monday. Durrance led the party of eight climbers, starting at 7:30 to make the climb in the face of sporadic icing and gusty winds. As crowds of spectators watched breathlessly from the foot of the Tower, the climbing party took until 3:45 that afternoon to reach the top.

The elated parachutist assured the climbers he would be able to climb back down as one of the party rather than having to be lowered as dead weight, providing they would show him the procedure. It took the party about four hours to descend, but the trip down was made without incident, even though the last couple of hours they were climbing in the dark, and floodlights were trained on the party to help their progress.

The crowd waiting at the bottom broke into cheers as the party of eight climbers and Hopkins finally reached the foot of the Tower, and the parachutist was greeted with tears of relief and hugs by many of the women in the crowd.

A rumor went around that the Wyoming Highway Patrolmen were waiting to whisk Hopkins away to Cheyenne, to reap the glory for Wyoming rather than letting him go back to Rapid City, but nothing came of the rumor, and after a brief news conference, Hopkins was taken to Brockelsby's home for his first night's rest away from his unique campsite in the sky.

In spite of the many air drops by pilot Clyde Ice, including quantities of food, water, extra clothes, bedding and tent, and even a pre-fabricated mini-house and stove arrangement, which failed to work, Hopkins was frequently shorted on some of the basics, primarily water. The planners could never figure out how to keep the containers from breaking, or popping off their lids, and he frequently obtained a drink from rain water of condensed moisture after a fog. Among one of the more useless items dropped to Hopkins was a load of coal from a Wyoming coal company.

During the Rapid City air fair Hopkins was unable to break the jump record afterall. He had hoped to jump in excess of the 30 jumps whch was then the record for the number made in a single day's time, but a combination of factors intervened. A stiff wind, one bad fall when a faulty chute only partially opened, and probably the debilitating effect of his Tower experience, all added up to a disappointing day for Hopkins, even though he managed to show the crowd 12 jumps, and most of those after the one in which he injured himself. The doctor treating him insisted upon his quitting the ordeal before he killed himself.

Not long after the Devil's Tower episode was over, Hopkins found himself in the exciting cloak and dagger action of the U.S. Secret Service, using his unique talents to experiment with new methods of dropping men and equipment behind enemy lines during World War II.

It was not until after the war that Hopkins finally married, and in 1958 he made his final parachute jump. Since then he has been content to live a subdued life in California as a construction engineer and father of four children.

The one thing that still puzzles Hopkins is why the big news surrounding the Devil's Tower incident was not the fact that a man could successfully manipulate his parachute through the tricky wind currents to land on the top, but that it took him so long to get the rest of the way down!

Footnote: Thanks are due Earl Brockelsby and his sister, Reta Mae Maierhauser, for the loan of materials concerning the Devil's Tower episode, and to author Dale M. Titler, whose chapter, *The* Man on Devil's Tower'' from his book, *Wings of Adventure* (Dodd, Mead—1970) was of much assistance in preparing the above article. J.J.

Photo Courtesy of Adrian Malone

Randy's Indian

Wayne Barton
Texas

On Thursday morning, Randy's Indian wasn't in his place. George Taylor was so surprised that he slowed the pickup truck, and even thought about stopping to look inside the cement culbert under the highway. He didn't, but did hitch up his sleeve to check the date on his calendar watch. Thursday, August sixth. The Indian should have been there.

Taylor pumped a cluster of oil leases for Wilburn Petroleum. He had driven the twenty-odd miles from his home to work five mornings a week for almost two years without being aware of the Indian, at least not as an individual. Now and then, he'd noticed Indians asleep along the shoulder where the Reservation butted up against the highway. Tom's Tom-A-Hawk Trading Post stood on the far side of the road, and some mornings, early in the month after the government checks came, there might be a dozen bodies scattered near there. But they had seemed as much a part of the landscape as the low red buttes. Then, one Saturday early in May, Taylor's five-year-old son had come out with him to hunt arrowheads.

That morning, there had been only one Indian. Randy saw him, curled beside a culvert a couple of hundred yards from the Tom-A-Hawk, his red shirt like a wound in the tall grass.

"Daddy, what's that man doing?"

Taylor followed the pointing finger and grinned. "He's asleep, Randy."

"Out there?" The boy's voice rose in disbelief. "Doesn't he have somplace to live?"

"I don't know. I guess he does. He's from the Reservation, across that fence."

"Is he an Indian?" Randy demanded. He climbed excitedly to his knees and peered out the rear window. "A real Indian?"

"Yes, he's an Indian."

"Well, maybe the soldiers shot him."

Taylor laughed, then saw Randy's hurt expression and reached across to pat his knee.

"I don't think so, Tiger. Say, how would you

103

like to see a badger's den? I found one last week, out behind the Number Ten well.''

After that, Taylor began to notice the Indian. He might be a few steps one way or the other, but his favorite spot seemed to be the grassy bank beside the culvert. He was always there the first ten or twelve days of the month. Then he would begin to skip days here and there, and he seldom showed up at all during the last week. Usually, he dressed in jeans and a faded western shirt, sometimes with a denim jacket. Around the first of the month, though, he wore his red shirt, with a high-crowned black hat and a belt of big overlapping silver conchos.

''I saw Randy's Indian again this morning,'' Taylor would tell his wife at supper. Or, ''Must be somebody's birthday. Randy's Indian was all dressed up.''

Randy's Indian was an institution in the Taylor household, and it was disturbing that an institution should change its habits on a cool August morning.

Taylor drove slowly as far as the Tom-A-Hawk's parking lot. No one was around. Even the low wooden steps in front of the door were vacant.

''Funny,'' Taylor said aloud. ''Guess he decided to stay home today.''

But it bothered him as he made his morning round of the wells and drove back to the pumper's doghouse to fill out his reports. Then at lunch, Stan Whittaker stopped by and reminded him.

''It's sure quiet out,'' Stan greeted Taylor. He perched on one corner of the scarred oak desk and began unpacking his lunchbox. ''I haven't seen a soul all day.''

''Mac 'll probably stop by later,'' Taylor said.

Stan snorted. ''He don't have to come out and play foreman with me. My wells are pumping all right.''

''Mack's not so bad. You get used to him.''

''Beats me why the Company won't put radios in these trucks. A radio's a lot of company, out like this.'' Stan ate in silence for a minute. ''Say, you put one in your truck yourself, didn't you?''

''Yeah, I got it at the junkyard and bolted it under the dash. Didn't cost much.''

''If I do that, will you help me put in in?''

''Well, sure.'' Taylor poured coffee. ''Be sure and get one that'll fit. It has to go in that little shelf.''

''Yeah. The wrecking yard out south of town has this Indian kid working there. I'll get him to find me one.''

Taylor paused in the act of peeling an orange and looked at Stan. ''An Indian, huh?''

''Yeah. He sure knows cars. The fellow that owns the place told me he'd run him off if he wasn't such a good mechanic.''

''Why's that?''

''Well, he'll come to work late, maybe nine or ten o'clock. Or if he feels bad or something, he might not show up at all for two-three days. No sense of time.''

''Sure,'' Taylor agreed, though he wasn't sure he did. Randy's Indian had never broken his pattern. He'd always been dependable. Taylor wiped his hands on his khakis and snapped his lunchbox closed.

''That makes me think of this Indian I know,'' he said. ''Well, I don't know him, really.''

And he told Stan the whole thing, about Randy and the trading post and the culvert, and about the Indian with the red shirt and the big black hat. It sounded silly to him as he talked, but Stan heard it though without laughing.

''I know how you feel.'' Stan said at the end.

''Well, I don't know. I just though it was funny, because he'd never missed a day this early in the month.''

Stan shrugged. ''Aw, you can't tell. Maybe his woman wouldn't let him out. Or maybe he stumbled into something and broke a leg.''

Once, Taylor had passed just as the Indian was waking up. It had been a cloudy morning, with a little chill in the air and the highway wet with dew. The Indian was sitting up, one leg doubled under him, the other thrust stiffly out in the grass. Driving past, Taylor caught an impression of a lean brown face with creases carved deep around the mouth. The Indian broke off a yawn to wave at the pickup, and Taylor waved back. It gave him a good feeling, as if the two of them shared a secret that morning.

''I hope nothing's happened to him,'' Taylor said.

He left the lease a little early, around four o'clock. He had hurried his final round, but half an hour wouldn't make much difference. Taylor wouldn't admit to himself that he had any plans, beyond having a drink at home and playing catch with Randy before supper. But he was worried, now, about the Indian.

As he neared the Tom-A-Hawk, he caught himself searching the shoulder of the road, looking for a patch of red. There were plenty of dry, rocky gullies for a man to fall into. The crazy so-and-so might even have been hit by a car. Maybe he was still out there someplace.

''Stupid,'' Taylor muttered to himself. Still he slowed the pickup when he came to the turnout for the trading post. He could go in and have a beer, maybe ask around. That wouldn't hurt anything. But it was none of his business.

He pressed the accelerator down and drove by, keeping his eyes on the highway. His resolve lasted until he had almost reached the culvert. Then he swore, swung the pickup into a wide U-turn, and drove back to park in front of the Tom-a-Hawk.

Taylor had never really looked at the place before. It was a low, sprawling wooden building, painted a hideous shade of green. The big windows were pasted with signs advertising Genuine Indian Jewelry and Huge Savings On Hand-Made Crafts. Off to one side was a pink house trailer, surrounded by beds of red and white petunias inside a low wire fence. There were two other cars in the parking lot, a battered Plymouth and a station wagon with New Jersey tags.

The sagging screen door groaned in protest as Taylor pushed through. To his right, the store opened out into a jumble of cabinets and shelves packed with cheap souvenirs. Near the door was a small case, crowded with silver-and-turquoise jewelry pawned by the people of the Reservation. A plump Indian girl watched indifferently while the New Jersey family prowled the aisles.

Taylor turned left through a narrow doorway labelled *Bar*—You Must Be 19. The proprietor looked up with a professional smile as he came in. Two Indians were playing bumper pool at a table in the back, while a third sat hunched in the dimness at the far end of the bar. Taylor pulled up a stool at the other end.

"Evening." The bartender was a small, stringy man with thinning white hair. "What'll you have?"

Now that he was inside, Taylor didn't know just what to say. "Beer. Nice day out."

"Oh, I reckon," the man agreed. He drew a glass of beer and set it down, then made change for Taylor's dollar bill.

"Had many tourists lately?"

"Oh, they come and go. There's a lot of time left in the season yet, a lot of time."

He glanced down the bar, went to make another drink for the seated Indian. Taylor waited. The bartender placed the glass in front of the Indian and came back.

"Matter of fact, those folks out there now are the only ones today. They bought some pottery—just junk."

"Taylor sipped his beer. "Yeah?"

"Oh, I used to carry a good line here. I know

turquoise, and a couple of women on the Reservation make good pottery. I had a contract in Arizona for rugs, Navajo rugs." He shrugged and waved a hand, indicating the New Jersey family and the world at large. "But they don't know the difference. All they want is junk."

Taylor nodded. "People are like that, I guess." He put his glass down. "Say, you must know a lot of the Reservation people."

"Oh, they come in, they have a drink, they go out. I been here fourteen years this coming October. Guess I've seen most of them."

"Yeah. I was looking for this one Indian. Wears a red shirt and a big black hat. I've seen him here sometimes, around the first of the month."

"Oh?" The other man's face closed a little. He picked up a rag and began wiping the bar. His eyes studied Taylor's grease-stained khakis.

"You're not from the law, I reckon. He owes you money or something, does he?"

"Nothing like that. No." Taylor tried to smile. "It's—well, I—I thought I might have a job for him. If he wanted it. But he didn't show up yesterday."

"Oh. A job."

"Nothing much. Just cleaning up around the place a little. I might do it myself."

Most of the suspicion left the man's face. He picked up the empty glass.

"Another beer?"

Taylor nodded. The bartender refilled the glass and set it carefully on the wet ring it had made on the bar.

"I might know who you mean. Red shirt, big hat. Does he have a bad leg?"

Taylor remembered the Indian sitting in the grass, his right leg rigid in front of him. "That's right."

"Oh, that's Jimmy Whitebird."

"Whitebird." It was funny, somehow, to think that Randy's Indian had a name, and maybe a family, and a life like other people.

"He'll probably be in later, if you want to see him. He comes in a lot the first part of the month. Gets a disability check from the government. I heard he got his leg hurt in Korea."

The bartender paused, studied the wall, looked back at Taylor.

"I'll tell you, he won't make too regular a hand. Drinks quite a bit. You know how they are, sometimes."

"No, I don't." The answer startled Taylor almost as much as the bartender. He groped for something else to say.

"I don't know how he is. Maybe he has his reasons."

The bartender stared for a moment, surprise and something else in his eyes. Then he nodded slowly.

"I guess that leg hurts him some," he said. He smiled for the first time, holding Taylor's eyes. "Might be enough reason for any man."

"Yeah." Taylor was uncomfortable. He'd already said too much, probably, but this was his chance. "Did he come in here yesterday?"

"Reckon not. I was closed."

"Closed?" Taylor sipped his beer, ducking his head to avoid the bartender's eyes. "Closed."

"Took the old lady in to the doctor. Wish I could find somebody to run the place when I'm gone. That girl's all right, but she can't tend bar."

"Yeah." Taylor drained his glass and stood up. "I better go. Thanks."

"Sure. Want me to tell Jimmy you were here?"

"No. No, I'll catch him later. Thanks."

Taylor drove home, feeling foolish and a little bit resentful. "I stopped at the trading post," he told his wife that night. "Just to look. He has some good turquoise."

The next morning, Randy's Indian lay curled in the tall grass near the culvert. His red shirt was stained, and the big hat was tipped far down over his face. Taylor grinned, feeling the world was as it should be again.

The Indian

Cynthia Jo Vannoy
Clearmont

The pale moon rises
shining its light
over the graves.

In the canyons the
ghost drums echo
for the dead.

Many died here,
spilled their blood
for freedom.

Now it's gone
passing, leaving
only aching memories.

Photo Courtesy of Nancy Bradberry

Land Twice Lost

Cynthia Jo Vannoy
Clearmont

The moon is a pale silver, the craters standing out sharply. Its light soothes the sleeping canyons and plateaus, turning them to soft gray and blue-white. In my ears I hear ghostly strains of tom-toms and Indian gourds. The music is wild and wilful, taking me back to the past.

Other people once lived here. People with bronzed skin and dark flashing eyes. People who lived their own lives and were happy with them. It's eerie, thinking that I may be standing on their bones. They are buried all over. With no headstones or tombs, many simply fell in battle and the land washed over them. What if these bones decided to rise again and take over the land of their fathers?

The hills recede into more hills, as I see them in the distance. Below me is the moonlit greasewood and sage-filled valley, sheltered by dark, forbidding hills and silver-yellow wheat fields. The hills are guardians, keeping vigil over the many bones and legends hidden within them. Battles were fought on these hillsides, and many scouts yelled for the hunters when a herd of buffalo showed their shaggy humps.

Now the shadows seem to take on human forms and whirl in one last ghostly dance for the dead, helped by the soft whispering of the prairie wind. The tom-tom beat grows wilder and more restless, and the spirits come at me with light ceremonial steps. A cloud covers the moon, mingling shadow into shadow and fading the ghost dancers into dust. Now they are gone—just as their human bodies went many years before.

Except for that one cloud, the rest of the blue-hued sky is clear, a promise of heat. The stars stand out clearly, looking like many campfires glowing out of a cold winter night.

I doubt if the Indians camped here much; there is no creek or spring to supply water for them or their animals. Maybe they galloped through here on their half-wild ponies, waving scalps or tenderly carrying wounded comrades. They may have treked through slowly, laden with travois and women, heading for a buffalo hunt or for new campgrounds.

Now, the only traces of their passing are a few arrowheads, scattered here and there. Perhaps this big one was left when a shaggy bull carried it as a stinging wound until he died, or did a hunter drop it as he crossed the country.

I feel close to the Indian. I ride the same country as he did, and my kinship with the land and nature is only a little less developed than his. My land, too, is being threatened as his was. No matter how hard he fought, his open range was destroyed by white man's progress. This newcomer killed off the buffalo and damned up the creeks. Soon, my open range will also be destroyed in the name of progress, and the rancher, too, will be only a ghostly figure of the distant past, like the Indian that he vanquished less than a century ago.

108

Photo Courtesy of Nancy Bradberry

Winter Roundup

Jean Goedicke
Casper

Strong winds
Chase, roll and toss
Tumble weeds into tight
Corners.

Those attempting
To escape
Are skewered on barbs
Held aloft
As examples to others—
Skeltons against the wind.

Those clearing fences
Hurl themselves
In leaps and bounds—
Wild mustangs
Determined
Not to be caught.

Photo Courtesy of Richard Kerwald

Wild Wyoming Wind

Lavinia Dobler
Riverton/New York

"She really loved life—with the kind of zest that comes down fresh from the mountains, on the wild Wyoming wind."

In a warm resonant voice, our neighbor of many years told of the confidence and enthusiasm Virginia Dobler Finigan, twin daughter of pioneers of the West, had given to others.

"As an Eastener myself," Austin Kiplinger continued, "I have to imagine that her zest for life has something to do with those streams that gush out of the valleys into upland prairies and wild sagebrush that surround Riverton, Wyoming, where she was born. I am sure that Virginia must have gotten it from her mother and father who settled out there nearly seventy years ago, giving their family the same love of life that they had themselves.

"She really loved life, and I think we ought to measure life by what it leaves. No material things, but the happiness, courage and faith that a life leaves for others. By this standard Virginia was a very rich woman."

Then our friends at the Memorial Service in Potomac, Maryland, having already received renewed strength and faith from the words of our neighbor as well as from those of our minister, experienced the spirit of the West when the organist played "Home on the Range." Although unsung, the words hummed through us...."And the skies are not cloudy all day." This song will

110

always have special meaning to those who heard it that April morning at St. Francis Episcopal Church.

A few days later the family, with Virginia, was flying westward, eager to reach those ageless mountains of Wyoming that signify continuity. I needed to be fortified once again by their changing beauty, by the strength and endurance they had given my twin and me in our growing up years.

Those snow-covered Wind River Mountains seemed to welcome us that clear, sunny morning when we stepped off the plane at Riverton.

Tumbleweeds raced across the highway as we faced those grand old mountains and then drove through the wrought-iron gate at Mountain View.

The wild Wyoming wind, fresh from those mountains, swirled around us as the Reverend Cross recited from memory the short but comforting Episcopal service: "I am the Resurrection and the Life..." The wind whipped his surplice as he made the sign of the cross, and looked out at the mountains.

Our hearts were sad, and there were tears, but our stepbrother, cousin, and our former schoolmates and friends of our pioneer parents shared with us the courage and strength Virginia and others have received from those majestic mountains.

I recalled our neighbor's words: "There is a special quality that some people have that others take strength from. It's a quality of outward-looking, towards friends and family, a quality of giving. Virginia had that quality. She gave something to everyone."

I thought of the encouragement and joy she had given her husband, her daughter and son, her grandchildren, her friends, countless strangers— and me.

I looked down at the wreath of sagebrush and white moss flowers and then towards the celestial mountains. I remembered more that our Maryland neighbor had said:

"When someone like Virginia moves on beyond this life, you have to give thanks for the qualities that she brought with her and passed on to the rest of us. That cheerful nature and her contagious laugh are for us to cherish. Lavinia, who started life at the same moment in time, can appreciate this more than all of the rest of us."

I heard a joyful sound. Was it the wild wind coming down fresh from the mountains, or my twin's bell-like laugh? I was filled with love and hope for all!

Virginia was home, near the mountains that had given her courage all her life. I glanced toward the adjoining land to the east—our father's homestead, now the site of Central Wyoming College. Students and their professors come often to the Dobler Reading Room.

By the hugh fireplace—made of jade, onyx, agate and other stones collected in that area by those who treasure Wyoming's prairies and mountains—young men and women often speak of their hopes and fears, and the future.

Through the windows they look out on the timeless mountains which will give them courage and appreciation for the beauty and purpose of life, and a reason for protecting and preserving them forever!

(Virginia Dobler Finigan, 1910-1975)

Over the gate leading into the Big Horn cemetery,
an iron sign reads:
  MOUNT HOPE WYOMING TERRITORY 1885

Photo Courtesy of Nancy Bradberry

Do They Care?

Nancy Bradberry
Sheridan

Do they care, sleeping now, on their sage strewn
  hillside
That we come back from time to time?
Hoping for that, we ourselves cannot find words
  for,
Knowing that what is here is not what we
  remember.
But still we come to stay a while,
To feel fresh wind across the open spaces,
To see the hills in order standing,
The earth's frame greening with another year.
Do they care when strangers, reading their fading
  dates,
Marvel at the courage they did not know they had?
"Times were not easy then or ever." they would
  have said.
"Women died borning children who, themselves,
  might die too young.
That was the way of it."
Do they know or care that we come back?
That we, so far from them in years, come back to
  honor them,
To thank them for being what they were
That we might follow their example?
Do they care, sleeping now, on their sage strewn
  hillside?

Photo Courtesy of Tessa J. Dalton

Haiku for Spring

Midge Swartz
Gillette

Loud hussy rain-drops
Clang gutters and startle me
After silent snow.

The cow's spring reward
Has clean hooves, earth brown body
And huge black calf eyes.

Anthem from the West

Mae Urbanek
Lusk

For one hundred and fifty-five years the United States had no national anthem! It was in an isolated South Dakota army post a few miles from the Wyoming border that action was begun to establish "The Star Spangled Banner" as the nation's official song.

The wife of Colonel Cabel H. Carlton, stationed at Fort Meade, South Dakota, in 1892 first suggested to her husband that he attempt to establish a special national song. A student of history, Colonel Carlton chose "The Star Spangled Banner" because of the stirring circumstances under which it had been written.

General Carlton wrote in 1914, "I was probably the first officer of the United States Army to order this air played at all band practices and to require all persons present to rise and pay it proper respect. Our printed programs for parades, band concerts, etc., stated that "The Star Spangled Banner" would be the last number played. A note at the bottom of the programs required all persons within hearing to rise, and all men not under arms to remove their hats.

The *New York Times* learned of this custom and printed a story telling how a cavalry colonel out on the South Dakota frontier was trying to establish a national anthem. Colonel Cook, then in command of the recruiting depot on David's Island on Long Island Sound, New York, corresponded with Colonel Carlton and then adopted his practice. Enthusing in his campaign, Carlton had an interview with Daniel E. Lamont, Secretary of War. Lamont was so impressed with the Colonel's idea that he issued an order requiring "The Star Spangled Banner" to be played at every army post each evening at retreat. In 1916 President Woodrow Wilson ordered it to be played on ceremonial occasions. But it was not until March 1931 that Congress finally passed a bill officially making "The Star Spangled Banner" the national anthem. The bill was signed by President Herbert Hoover.

The tune was first popular as a drinking song in Germany, France and England. In 1775 John

Stafford Smith, a composer for the Royal Chapel, wrote new lyrics to it praising an ancient Greek poet, Anacreon. The tune soon became known in America and words criticising President John Adam's foreign policy were written to it, and known as "Adams and Liberty." In 1807 another set of lyrics was written praising American officers leading a campaign against Mediterranean pirates. These words were composed by a Baltimore lawyer and amateur poet named Francis Scott Key.

Then America again went to war with England. The Red-coats set Washington aflame and forced President Madison to flee the White House. In September 1814 a British fleet sailed into Chesapeake Bay to attack Fort McHenry, a citadel of Baltimore. William Beanes, a Baltimore physician, was held prisoner on one of the British ships. Accompanied by an American prisoner-exchange officer, Francis Scott Key rowed out to the fleet to request the release of his doctor friend. The request was granted, but the men were told they would have to remain on board during the planned attack.

"Look at your flag tonight," a British officer taunted Key. "Tomorrow it will be gone." The flag flying over Fort McHenry had fifteen stars and had been sewed from bunting by Mrs. Mary Young Pickersgill and her two nieces.

The attack began. For hours British shells raked the fort. In the gunfire Key saw Old Glory still flying. When the bombardment stopped a heavy fog lay over the bay. Key could not see the flag.

Perhaps the battle—perhaps American independence was over!

Through the early hours Key desperately watched for some sight of the flag. Then, finally, dawn revealed the Stars and Stripes still flying. Taking an old envelope from his pocket, in wild poetic joy, Key started writing. He continued to jot down words even while he and his friends were being taken back to shore. That night he finished the words that fitted the stirring tune to which he had written another poem. The song, though difficult to sing, soon became widely popular but had no official recognition.

The flag that inspired the anthem is now at the Smithsonian Institution in Washington D.C. British bullets had torn it in eleven places. One corner of the banner is missing, too. Possibly it was used to fulfill the request of a soldier that his body be shrouded in a piece of the flag he died defending.

Another Star Spangled Banner floats continually over the grave of Francis Scott Key in Frederick, Maryland. He died in 1843 without knowing how great was his contribution.

Fort Meade, South Dakota, is now a Veterans Administration Hospital, and the memory of army men who were stationed there—Custer, Reno, Stugis and Carlton is preserved in street names, in a museum, and in legend. The flag still flies each day over the parade ground where the "Star Spangled Banner" was first used as an official song.

Illustration Courtesy of Chip Wood

Far Away Drum

Peggy Simson Curry
Casper

There must be words if their rhythm be bold
And built like a log corral,
There must be words to catch and to hold
Wyoming in like an outlaw horse,
But they are not mine. I cannot keep
A land where the savage is never asleep
But wary and slipping the noose of mind;
Something the heart cannot name though it find
And feel like the throb of a far-away drum.

There must be words if their rhythm be wide
And spiked like a silver spur,
There must be words to saddle and ride
Wyoming down like an outlaw horse.
My lips shape thoughts gone thin and cold,
Like a wagon-wheel sound
On a moon white stone.
The long creeks loop the hills with frost,
The far-away drum-beats drift the plains.
Echo away—and are lost.

There must be words in the big wind's talk
With rhythms sharp as a soapweed spear,
Words mustang wild and Indian-savage,
Cowboy-proud and profane as a pioneer.
I spread my mind like a barbed wire fence
To catch them like tumbleweed, hold them fast.
But Wyoming is gone—
Stampeding in distance
And I hear the wild hoofbeats come
Out of the dusk—like a far-away drum.

Reprinted by permission of author

Fort Caspar

Peggy Simson Curry
Casper

Here flows the Platte, no longer loud and wild
But disciplined by man and passive in its bed.
Here is the Fort, grown shabby as the sage.
Dust from the Fair Grounds falls on trees
Where Indian and soldier knelt to ease
The pain of wounds, and westward on the plain
The redmen and the white fell side by side.
Earth holds their bones impartially;
Wind strokes the range grass where they died.

The city grows from dreams and dust,
From the hard brown hands of men,
From women's heartbreak and from love—.
The slow Platte wears the city's stain;
Refineries rise to split the wind,
Belching their strange, rank breath upon the air.
The old Fort stands in silence and apart,
Wrapped in the story that is history;
Within it beats the city's dreaming heart.

Photo Courtesy of Archie Nash

Parade of the Clippity Clops

Charles W. Popovich
Sheridan

CLIPPITY CLOP the horses trot
  echoes on the pavement
where once there was the barren sod,
  before the westward movement.

When the cities sprouted and grew
  from people moving west,
then out went the useful horses,
  along with much of the rest.

Now all that continues to be
  recalling other days
Is CLIPPITY CLOP as horses trot
  in the annual parade.

The Man Who Laughed Well

Mary Alice Gunderson
Casper

His humor was known from coast to coast, but Bill Nye's career began in a small Wyoming town.

"We can never become a nation of snobs so long as we are willing to poke fun at ourselves," he wrote in a newspaper column. "It saves us from making asses of ourselves...I always like to tell anything that has the general effect of turning the laugh on me because then I know that there will be no hard feelings."

Armed with belief that he could write, down to his last quarter and dime and a peeling yellow cardboard suitcase, Edgar Wilson Nye arrived in Laramie City, Wyoming Territory, in May, 1876. Back home in Wisconsin he had worked in a mill, been village schoolmaster and failed the bar exams twice. "...in those days everybody who wore a big hat and got tired easily with manual toil was set aside for ministry or the law," Nye wrote. "There was a time...when people thought that I ought to be 'admitted' (to the bar)...Every spring and fall term I would go through this ordeal, and then get bound over for examination the following term. Finally it got to be part of the calendar."

Though he had done only a little writing, his first job in the West was Assistant Editor of the LARAMIE SENTINEL. A two-man operation edited by Dr. J.H. Hayford, the SENTINEL averaged a scant four pages with short articles sandwiched between ads for horse linament and miracle salves. Nye's lively essays were definite improvements. One of his early columns described Laramie—then a few hundred brick and frame buildings huddled around the railway station—as a place where "the altitude is high, the assessed valuation low; liquor is plentiful, water scarce."

Before his first year in the Territory was out, twenty-five year old Bill Nye had passed the bar, hung out his shingle and married Miss Fannie Smith. "One evening while the town lay hushed in slumber..." he wrote, "I moved. Not having any

Sketch of Bill Nye by Fred Opper

Reprinted from Bill Nye's Western Humor, by T.A. Larson, by permission of University of Nebraska Press, Lincoln, Nebraska, 1968.

piano or sideboard, I did the moving myself. It did not take long." About the time of his marriage Nye's columns began to receive national attention

Easily recognizable, Nye's style was one of rapid change, all-stops-out exaggeration, perhaps reflecting the character of the land itself—its rugged mountains, snowcapped year round; broad plains, swept by severe late spring blizzards; gullies cut by cloudbursts that cleared to sunny skies in a matter of hours. But not far under the surface of Nye's most outlandish statement lurked a truth.

Despite his growing popularity, his boss was dissatisfied. Dr. Hayford preferred factual, down-to-earth reporting, Nye admitting that he could "write up things that never happened with a masterly and graphic hand. Then, if they occur afterward, I am grateful; if not, I bow to the inevitable and smother my chagrin." He quit the paper after about eighteen months, ran unsuccessfully for the legislature, then tried to support himself as a lawyer.

Carried in papers ranging from TEXAS SIFTINGS to the DETROIT FREE PRESS, Nye caricatured himself as a lawyer. "While I was called Judge Nye. . .I was out of coal about half the time and once could not mail any letters because I did not have the necessary postage," he claimed.

". . .while I had some of the prerequisites of a lawyer I lacked the one great essential, and that is the ability to repeat a law, a ruling or a definition in the exact language of anybody else."

Over the next several years Nye also served as justice of the peace and U.S. Commissioner though the salaries added little to his income. "I was also ex-officio coroner. I would marry a quick-tempered couple in the morning, sit on the husband in the afternoon, and try the wife in a preliminary way in the evening for the murder."

Often writing in the privacy of his too quiet law office, Nye advised Eastern readers: "Let no man from a large Eastern city console himself with the notion he is conferring favor on the West by removing himself to that part of the country...He who goes west solely to teach the untutored pioneer the elements of refined civilization will not endear himself to his community...In the West *America* sticks out more prominently...To succeed in the West a young man must become a part of his adopted country and be loyal to it..."

Nye took his own advice; his columns spelled out the time spent picnicing, fishing the clear mountain streams, camping in the Medicine Bow Range. He named his gold and silver mines, too optimistically, "New Jerusalem" and "The Vanderbilt."

Once he mused, "I could be poor and come nearer to enjoying it in the West than anywhere else..." His family doubled in size with the arrival of two daughters, Bessie and Winnie.

But one hundred fifty dollars a month and editorship of a new, Republican-backed paper was a boon to the struggling young family. First issue of the BOOMERANG, named for Nye's "narrow gauge mule" which had become his mascot, came out in March, 1881. The BOOMERANG carried a full AP report and soon became the most widely quoted paper in the West. Critics of the paper said it was named that because so many copies came back.

Eugene Field, James Whitcomb Riley and Bill Nye at the time of their lecture appearance at Indianapolis in 1886.

Photo Courtesy of Mary Alice Gunderson

To these critics Nye explained, "The BOOM-ERANG has been charged with erring...and coloring things a little too high. There is an excuse for lack of spice...in the newspaper world. The men who write for our dailies...have to write about two miles a day, and ought not to be kicked if it is not interesting. We have done some 900 miles of writing ourself during our short, sharp and incisive career...Those things we wrote at a time when we were spreading our graceful characters over ten acres of paper per day were not thrilling. They did not catch the public eye, but were just naturally consigned to oblivion's bottomless maw...Excellence is what we seek, not bulk. Write better things and less of them, and you will do better, and the public will be pleased to see the change."

Later he charged potential readers of his work to "take a little at a time. If you read it all at once and it gives you the heaves, you deserve it."

Besides personal affairs, Nye's work presented home-grown, grass roots opinions popular in the West. Occasionally he spoke through a fictitious character such as Elias Kilgore, retired stage driver, speaking to the Legislature on the subject of woman suffrage. "It's _____ funny to me that woman who suffers most in order that man may come into the world...the one that is first to find and last to forsake Him, was first to hush the cry of a Baby Savior in a Jim Crow livery stable in Bethlehem and last to leave the Cross, first at the sepulchre and last to doubt the Lord, should be entrusted with the souls and bodies of generations and yet not know enough to vote."

His essay, "Petticoats at the Polls, ended succinctly: "We don't know what the Territory would have been without female suffrage, but when they began to hang men by law instead of by moonlight, the future began to brighten up."

Of the so-called mail order brides Bill Nye admitted that "Wyoming wants women, and wants them bad, but there is no very clamorous demand for sentimental fossils who want a bonanza husband and a pass from the effete East."

Mourning the passing of the frontier, he noted that "building railroads has knocked the essential joy out of the life of a pioneer...It has driven out the long handled frying pan and the flapjack of twenty years ago, and introduced the condensed milk and canned fruit of commerce...the modern camp is not the camp of the wilderness...You know that if you ride a day you will be where you can get the daily papers and read them under the electric light...The road is lined with empty beer bottles and peach cans that have outlived their usefulness."

Nye's harsh parallel, "The Rocky Mountain Hog," spelled out the contemporary attitude toward the Indian and the intolerance we have only partially overcome. He wrote "Civilize the hog. Build churches and school houses for him. Educate him and teach him the ways of industry...the hog of the present is but a poor, degraded specimen of the true aboriginal hog, before civilization had encroached upon him... once he was pure as the beautiful snow..."

But Nye's position softened a few years later. A poignant scene framed by the window of a pullman car haunted him, and he wrote, "I've never been a pronounced friend of the Indian...I have claimed that though he was first to locate in this country, he did not develop the lead or do assessment work even, so the thing was open to relocation...the Indian is shiftless day and night...But when we see the poor devils buying our coffins for their dead, even though they may go hungry for days afterward, and, as they fade away forever as a people, striving to conform to our customs and wearing suspenders and joining in prayer, common humanity leads us to think solemnly of their melancholy end."

Only occasionally did Nye's prejudice narrow to focus on one individual. Most often described as a warm companion and steadfast friend, he could also be quick tempered and impulsive. His description of a woman at a fancy dress ball as "painted up like a sutler wagon" earned threats from her husband. Another time he laid low at a friend's ranch on the Big Laramie River until a man he had called a liar in his column cooled off.

Relations with his former editor, Dr. Hayford, continued cold and the two men took frequent pot shots at each other in their papers. Hayford was a fervid promoter of the Territory and in one SENTINEL editorial wrote that Laramie City is "the only one of all the towns in this region which is almost entirely exempt from hard winds...The blustering storms and howling winds spend their fury harmlessly in the mountains around us and above, while perpetual calm and sunshine bless the inhabitants below."

Nye countered with one of his more quoted essays: "It has snowed a good deal during the week (in July) and it is discouraging to the planters of cotton and tobacco very much...the climate (in Laramie) is erratic, eccentric and peculiar. The altitude is between 7,000 and 8,000 feet above the high water mark, so that during the winter it does not snow much, we being above the snow line, but in the summer the snow clouds rise above us and (the agriculturist) is virtually compelled to wear his snow shoes all through his haying season...Early frosts make close connections with late spring blizzards.''

Nowhere is it recorded what Hayford's reaction was when Bill Nye, still editor of the BOOMERANG, was appointed postmaster, a position Hayford had held for six years. Nye continued his newspaper work but delegated many of his post office duties. His first play, ''The Cadi'', evolved from some of his post office experiences as did a number of other essays.

Of post office traffic Nye said that the ''official count shows that only two and a half percent of those who to go to the post office transact their business and then go away. The other 97 and one half per cent do various things to cheer up the post master and make him earn his money...There is an amusing party who cheerfully stands up against the boxes and reads his letters, and laughs...or swears when the letter doesn't suit him...There is a woman who skittishly chides the clerk because she doesn't get her letter. He good naturedly tells her, as he has done daily for seven years, that he will write her one tomorrow...''

''I believe the voting class to be divided into two parties...those who are in the postal service and those who are mad they cannot receive a registered letter every 15 minutes of each day, including Sunday.''

In addition to his postmaster's salary, his salary at the BOOMERANG and income from syndicated columns, Nye was also receiving royalties from his first two books, published at Laramie—*Bill Nye and Boomerang* and *Forty Liars and Other Lies*. A third book, *Baled Hay*, (called by author a ''drier book than *Leaves of Grass*'') was being assembled. Nye and two associates were finalizing plans to purchase a more up-to-date printing press in a push for still wider circulation. Subscriptions to the BOOMERANG were pouring in from many parts of the United States.

Suddenly in the fall of 1882 Nye was struck down by a serious illness. Delirious with a raging fever, he was treated by the family doctor for pneumonia, then ''inflammatory rheumatism.'' For three months he lay ill at home with little improvement. During a break in the February weather the Nyes and their two young daughters moved a few belongings to Greeley, Colorado, to stay with his wife's relatives. Bitter toward the Laramie doctor, Nye wrote later ''...one day I arose during a temporary delirium and extracting

a slat from my couch, I smote (the doctor) across the pit of the stomach with it while I hissed, 'Physician, heal thyself!' ''

Cerebro-sinal meningitis was the Greeley Physician's diagnosis—cranial nerve damage with no hope of a permanent cure for the recurring severe muscle spasms, the weakened eyes. Fearing addiction, Nye usually refused the morphine prescribed for his blinding headaches. Told he must live at a lower elevation, Bill Nye gained strength over the summer and returned to Laramie to settle some debts and resign the postmastership. Without him the BOOMERANG shrank to just another small town paper.

''No sooner does man become wealthy than he at once develops some kind of high priced disease. This is not alone my experience, but it is also the experience of other wealthy men. Wealth always costs all the assessor counts it at, and often more,'' he wrote.

Nye returned in 1883 to his native Wisconsin, before he left clipping all of his columns from BOOMERANG files. He left behind him health, business responsibilities, participation in politics and his finest work.

But his reputation survived several years of semi-retirement and in 1885 the BOSTON GLOBE and NEW YORK WORLD took up his new column. Soon sixty papers across the land carried his essays. By the early 1890's he was the nation's best known, highest paid humorist, earning more than $30,000 a year from books, columns and lectures.

Nye's post-Laramie affluence contrasts sharply with the lean Wyoming years. The uncertainty of his health—plus the desire to provide for his wife, two daughters and the two sons, born in Wisconsin—prodded him to undertake a series of exhausting, coast-to-coast lecture tours. Recurrent bouts with meningitis caused some cancellations each season and sometimes left him too weak to write at all.

Though he owned a Staten Island townhouse and an estate deep in the North Carolina hill country, he was often on the road for months at a time. His reputation spreading, he played to increasingly larger audiences; most popular of all his programs were those based on his life in the West.

Still meeting his weekly deadline for his newspaper column, Nye wrote in train compartments, hotel rooms, dressing rooms in theaters, and opera houses. When critics—he called them ''old fashioned, brocaded, base-burning critics''—panned him for quantity of work rather than quality, he replied that he would continue so long as his publisher and his public demanded it, and "so long as I must stare the flour barrel in the face."

All told, his work appeared in 14 volumes under twenty titles. He wrote an estimated 3 million words for publication in addition to some fifty personal letters a week. For twenty years he contributed stories to COSMOPOLITAN, CENTURY, LADIES' HOME JOURNAL and COLLIER'S.

Nearly a decade of success on the platform ended tragically in Paterson, New Jersey, November, 1895. Weakened by a series of slight strokes, Nye stumbled mounting the stage and was unable to begin. Believing him to be drunk, the audience pelted him with rotten eggs as he left the theater. It was his last performance. Shortly before Christmas his play, "The Stag Party," folded after two weeks on Broadway.

On a bleak day in January, 1896, Bill Nye penned his last personal letter to his brother, Frank, from his home in Carolina. "...how many mirages we see before we actually lay our hands upon the real and true," he wrote.

In mid-February Nye suffered a last severe stroke, lapsing into a coma. On Washington's Birthday, 1896, Bill Nye died; he was 46. A month after his death a third son was born to Mrs. Nye.

For his monument at Calvary Episcopal Church in Fletcher, North Carolina, the family chose this inscripion: "I will turn their mourning into joy and will comfort them and make them rejoice from their sorrow."

There is no monument in Wyoming marking the years Nye spent here.

His life had been for many years an open book to people all around the nation. Most moving of all the tributes received by his family is one from an anonymous reader who never met Bill Nye, but knew him well. "He made men laugh because he himself knew how to laugh, and few men know how to do that...Many people believe that humor is shallow. Laughter and tears lie very close together, and that man who laughs well is easiest moved to tears...no humorist is ever shallow."

Related information was researched from Bill Nye biographical and miscellaneous newspaper files, Hebard Room, Western Archives and Historical Research Center, University of Wyoming, Laramie, Wyoming.

Photo Courtesy of Archie Nash

Intolerance is Forever

Gladys B. Beery
Laramie

The horsemen were poised at the brow of the valley, grim black shapes in the pale light. A bit-chain rattled, leather creaked. A horse blew noisily, pawed impatiently. The riders stared in angry silence at the white blur below which marked the herder's wagon, and at the larger blur marking the bedded-down sheep.

Wind, for patient centuries, had worn and shifted the soil, molding this long valley. It lay at an angle to the towering snow-swept mountains, gently sloped, well watered, dressed with thick grasses, a thousands-acre prize.

The full moon swung high above the western peaks. In the soft flood of moonlight, shadows lay over the long slopes of land and traced the wandering course of the stream along the bottom of the valley. Darker shadows marked clumps of trees and brush. Here and there silver glinted where moonlight touched water.

Although the men had reached their decision, they seemed reluctant, uneasy, putting off action. They were honest men, hard working. They felt that their actions leading up to this moment had been more than fair and just.

Strong among them ran the memory of their neighbor's words. They had gone asking him to join in this thing which they felt necessary.

"No, I won't go. These things can get out of hand all too easy."

"Out of hand! It ain't gonna get out of hand. All we're gonna do is dirty up his camp and move him over the hill. There ain't gonna be any rough stuff, we'll see to that. Hell, man—we're reasonable! You know that. And we been patient, too. But we've sure reached the end of our patience!''

"Yep. I know all that. You're reasonable when you're cool. But you're plenty well riled now. Go home. Cool off, and then come back.''

"Cool off! Hell, man! We go home and think it over, and the more we think about it—why man, then we will get mad. And let that little son-of-a-shriveled up baboon set and spread his sheep stink over the entire country, trampin' grass into the ground. He's on my land, Ben. Land I need. And he's ruinin' it for cattle graze. I want him off.''

"Your land? All proved up?''

Silence. Scuffling of boots, shifting bodies.

"You can't push him out, Harry. He's your neighbor. A neighbor's got rights, too. Let him live, too.''

"Rights hell!'' Temper flaring again. "What about mine? What about ours? Let him in and the country'll be over-run with 'em. Rights? Don't any of us have rights, too?'' Impatience in his every line. "Come on along and let's straighten him out.''

"No.'' A touch of sorrow in his voice. "Not me. I won't be involved in this. Go on if you want.''

They had left in impatient disgust, muttering their reactions. Now, as they stared into the moonlit valley: "It belongs to us and the cattle,'' the big man stated in a justifying tone. "We was here first. We did the fightin' and the diein' and the buildin' work. We tamed this land and won it. And this damned whinin' sheepherder comes along—and sets down—it ain't right. He ain't got no claim—.''

The man blew his nose, then grunted. "It ain't that I got personal objections to him—I guess even sheepherder's gotta live, too. But they can damn well live somewheres else. They ain't nothin' wrong with 'em—long's they keep their place.'' Another pause, then: "An that place damn well ain't near me.''

Clouds scudded across the sky, dimming the bright moon and star shine. An' early spring breeze stirred and hastened over the long land combing the new grass, whispering along the slopes ahead of danger.

The big man spat largely. "Oh, dammit!'' he blurted.

The night quiet was suddenly shattered by the sharp call of a coyote and from toward the mountains floated back a thin, lonely reply. The breeze-filled quiet again settled down.

"Well, then, let's get on. Standin' here looking' down at him ain't settlin' anything—or gettin' him outa the country!'' one of the men said sharply.

There passed among them a sound like a sigh, a sort of uneasy shame. The group stirred. There came a slap of reins, chirrup to horses, then the roll of hoofbeats drummed into the night.

From the camp below there came the sharp, questioning bark of dogs, their quick staccato of alarm. The breeze ran ragged, shifted, carrying the certain sound of the running horses upon the camp. There was a stir down there.

A shadow detached itself from the wagon, stood spraddle legged in the bright moonlight, rifle plainly in sight. Clamoring dogs fell abruptly

silent. The night was filled with the thunder of running horses and the sudden, spiteful tattoo of gunshots.

The sheep stirred in confusion, blatting, then leaped to their feet as gunshots stitched among them and were gone into the night pursued by lead and the frantic dogs trying to hold them. Their plaintive alarm thinned into the night as the wooley mass streamed across the valley.

Thunder of gunfire rolled along the slopes, echoed long against the far mountains. A voice shouted almost hysterically, "Dammit, we told you—you bastard—no place for you here.."; the scream of a struck horse, crack of a rifle; spit of sixguns; rattle of shots against the wooden sides of the white canvas-topped wagon.

The tensions charged swiftly, became charged, hot with anger. The surging and shouting and shooting grew. The wagon canvas was riddled, long tatters flapping.

A loop snaked out and over the head and shoulders of the lone defender, pinning his arms tightly to his sides. Everyone had forgotten the neighbor's warning that "things would get out of hand." A second rope settled about his neck, men shouted, horses surged toward the nearest trees.

As the man's squirming body was hauled upward, another rope was tossed and caught the wagon, pulling it to the ground, adding to the racket and dust. The man's resisting body reached the peak of its climb; the feet gave one great kick and hung still, in limp protest to unreason.

From the shattered wagon came the shrill hysterical screams of a small child. By the light of the now cloudless moon the man saw the child beside the quiet, flung body of a woman.

The child screamed on and on into a sudden shuddering silence.

"My God!" the big man voiced their frozen horror. "What have we done? We was only goin' to scare him out of the country!"

They all turned stiffly to stare at the body of the sheepherder turning now slowly against the light of the impersonal moon.

A flock of cranes fluted into the northern sky, and the wind cried small in the treetop, cried for the age-old unchanging hurt done by unthinking passion.

I Remember

Marcia W. Hoffman
Jackson

Illustration Courtesy of Chip Wood

He was quite a spry buckskin with long, flowing mane
And the look in his eye made it perfectly plain
He was wiry and quick, prob'ly mean to the core
And so proud that he'd never been ridden before,

Then a cowboy walked up, without blinking an eye;
He looked the horse over and thought he might try
To subdue this old pony, all yellow and black
And we all held our breaths as he eased on his back.

With a snap that was deaf'ning they spun round and round;
With a snort the old horse drug his nose on the ground;
His wild eyes rolled back and he bit at the feet
Of the stranger who rode sitting tight in his seat.

For the young cowboy sat there just like he was glued
And we all knew from THEN on, this kid was no dude.
When the dry dust had settled, the buckskin was through—
It appeared he had just learned a lesson or two.

So the two became friends and for day after day
Where the ONE was, the other was not far away.
The pony had cow sense, and willingness too
There just wasn't much that he COULDN'T do!

The buckskin still stands in his very own place;
The varnish has peeled from his neck and his face,
But we still can recall with a great deal of pride
The day that our two-year-old broke him to ride.

Reprinted from
THE WESTERN HORSEMAN

A Cup Of Coffee

Thomas Connell
Lander

I left the car just where it was;
A rancher's house was not too far away.
I could walk there for help.
    The rancher waited in the yard as I approached.
Quite unpretentiously his youth had slipped away,
Leaving a shell of covered bones
and thin bowed legs
From hours in the saddle.
    He listened as I spoke. Then said
"I'm here alone, except for Maw.
But I could get the pickup, I suppose
And take you to the Millers.
They've got a phone."
    I noticed that his lips had twitched
As humor sparked his eyes.
"You know, it's not so long ago
I'd a hitched a team to take you there
or gone horseback."
    But turning then to go,
He stopped and said
"A cup of Java wouldn't go so bad
Right now. If you don't mind the wait.
What little time we lose
Won't make no difference, no how."
    Seated in the kitchen
We sipped the steamy drinks.
"This house is new," he volunteered,
"As you can see. Both Maw and me
Had dreamed of one like this.
But every time we thought we could.
We couldn't. Something happened.
Twice it was hard winter storms
That crimped us so bad.
Another time 'twas Maw.
Every cent that we could raise
We used to make her well
And bring her back to us,
Then there was kids to raise
And send to school.
We never got it done till now."
    He looked about the room
With modest pride
And maybe resignation.
"But now we're old. We just don't need
Such fancies anymore.
I don't know why we built it
Now, at all. More to prove, I guess,
That we could do it."
    He pointed to some photographs
Upon a trim buffet.

"Those are our girls, June and Nancy.
Nancy is the little one. She died
When just thirteen. Fell off a horse
And never did come to.
Wasn't much that we could do.
Too far to get a doctor here in time.
    "June lives in San Francisco now.
She's married; has three kids.
Both she and Gilbert work at jobs,
With debt up to their ears.
Trying to have their cake
And eat it too, I guess.
    "The two upon the left,"
(he pointed with his thumb),
"Are our two boys. John's the one in G.I. clothes.
The other one is Jim."
    His eyes grew pensive as his finger
Traced the cup's smooth lip.
"John always was hot-tempered.
Him and me, we never got along too well.
Maw blames it most on me.
She may be right. I didn't understand
The boy, I guess.
    "We had our final quarrel
The day before he joined the Marines.
I signed his papers
'Cause he wasn't quite eighteen.
Maw cried, of course. But I said
'He's got to learn the world's not made
For him alone. He'll learn it there."
    The rancher paused a moment,
Then he said, "He's gone.
Killed, fighting in Korea.
Been gone since fifty-two."
    The cups were filled again.
With thoughts still in the past
He said, "We had a dog. A collie.
Big and bright and proud
He really was John's dog.
But we all claimed him, more or less.
He'd work for John or Maw,
But for the rest of us
"Twas only if he wanted to.
But after John was gone
He palled along with me.
A right good hand he made then, too.
I had him with the sheep
The day before we got the word
That John was dead."
    The old man paused again
Gazing into the past.
And then he said, "This is how it was.
Coyotes had been bothering
So I kept the rifle handy, by the bunk.

The night was partly cloudy,
Partly dark and light.
I was tense, I guess. Had a feeling
All along that something wasn't right.
So when the bells all started ringing
And the sheep began to blat
I jumped up and with the rifle in my hand
Looked out the wagon door.
    "The moon was just a-showing past a cloud
And the ridge beyond the bed-ground
Glowed in fuzzy light.
And there I thought a coyote moved
Against the moon-lit sky."
    The memory seemed to chafe.
He rubbed his cheek and chin.
"Any other time I would have missed!
I fired without aiming, and shot Duke.
I forgot how he would circle
The whole band each time
The sheep got restless or disturbed.
    "Dogs work their way into your heart,"
He said, "But more than that,
Because he was John's dog,
He was our tie with John.
    "I couldn't leave him there
To rot like any piece of carrion.
So I dug a grave and buried him
And built a pile of stones
To mark the spot.
    "The next day Hank Miller came
To let me know 'bout John.
"I was up to where I buried Duke last week,
Looking for a mare that we'd lost.
I don't know why, but somehow
I couldn't quite resist on seeing how
Old Duke was making out.
I found the grave all right
But the rocks had fallen down."
    He stopped his reminiscing then and said,
"The past is past. There's nothing we can change.
The other boy is Jim, as I have said.
He's a captain in the Air Force now
And flies a jet. He's married, too,
With two little girls, cute as they can be.
We never see him very much,
And he very seldom writes."
    I mentioned then, to lighten if I could
The conversation's tones, "He's riding higher
    now
Than Dad, and over wider ranges."
    The old man smiled, but slightly,
"I guess he is, I've thought about it
Times when I've been skirting Sheep Ridge
On a hunt. A fellow can't feel too important
Way up there."

He pointed out a window.
"That's Sheep Ridge knifing sharply to the right.
From there it's glacier country.
Thirteen thousand feet. But that's just fetlock
   high
To forty thousand feet."
   And so I said, "He's up a little closer
To the stars, and maybe, even God."
I meant it as a jest, but it fell flat.
It sounded merely silly and inane.
   However, the old man seemed not to mind.
He nodded as he said, "I just don't know.
Ain't none of US been too successful there,
I guess. Too many hates and taints.
I guess it ain't exactly where you're at
That counts."
   Then pushing back his chair he said,
"We'll get to the Millers now, I guess."
   But outside on the kitchen steps he paused
To watch a jet-stream arch the vast blue sky.
"I like to think, sometimes," he said,
"It's Jim up there." He shook his head.
"But I know it likely ain't."

Reprinted from IN WYOMING
Mar. - Apr. 1974

This poem was first place winner in the Wyoming
Writers contest in 1974.

Snowbirds

Midge Swartz
  Gillette

Yeah, we see them come every year
starting October and gone by May.
Arizona is western
if you know what I mean
But those old Wyoming ranchers
well, they're a different breed
of western.
Even in tie shoes and sport jackets
you can see their tooled belts
peeking out.
Years of pitching hay and tamping posts
make them look sorta stuffed
into those city clothes
and they roll high heeled
whether wearing them or not.
They act like they never seen
a tree before
let alone an orange grove
and they look at everything
like it's far away.
They're like kids
wanting to see and try
and do it all
now that their work's done.
Chamber of Commerce says
they bring money
but that ain't all they bring.

Photo Courtesy of Emmie Mygatt

132

Here Blind We Walk

Thomas Connell
Lander

Here blind we walk; our ethnic past
bound tight about our eyes; if there is more
than this in sight, we can not know.
Our beacon is a shadow cast, and we unknowing,
See the way to go, destined to think
that here are all the skies, and all there is
    of light.